Chapter 1

EMILY

The year was 1931. The place was Anywhere, USA. What would be called The Great Depression 60 years later, was just called 'hard times' now. The woman was sitting in the old car beside the road with a forlorn look on her face. Hope looked like it might have dwelt there once but was now long gone.

Actually, it was called Perryville, Kentucky and it just happened to be where the old Ford had decided to quit running. She had opened the door and heard a hissing noise. Despair hadn't hit her full force yet so she gave a dry laugh and said to herself, "I guess it decided to have a flat tire, too." Her humor quickly gave way to reality, and reality was that she was all out of tire patches and money. Not only that, but the boy and girl sitting in the back seat with large eyes wondering what was coming next, would probably have to go to sleep hungry tonight. She thought she had a couple of slices of bread in the food box but that wasn't much and she knew that they would insist on sharing with her.

She had hoped to be in Redhouse, Virginia before they were terribly hungry but that was an impracticality now. Her sister lived at Redhouse, and she and her husband grudgingly offered them refuge. Not that they didn't like her but they had a young child of their own and like people all over the country, they were having 'hard times', too. The only difference was that they were on a farm and had a garden and six cows that brought them in a small milk check every two weeks.

Her name was Emily Jones and the children were Joey, 8 years old, and Ruthie, 6 years old. Her husband, Harlan, had left home walking toward California over a year ago with a promise that when he reached the Golden Land of Opportunity named California, he would send for her and the kids. The old car had been out of commission when he left or he probably would have taken it and them with him. He had been a good husband and she had trusted him to do what he said he would do. But it had been over a year with no word from him and she had begun to lose hope that she ever would know what had happened to him. A man like Harlan had a lot of pride and it hurt him deeply not to be able to support his family.

She had let the neighbor boy, Irwin, tinker with the Ford and miraculously; he had put it in working shape again. In return she had given him a ride to Galt's Landing, Kentucky. She had dropped him off about an hour ago and sorely wished she still had him with her. She and Irwin had patched 6 flat tires since they had left Wolf Creek, Illinois, six days ago. They had found a grassy spot at night and rolled up in a blanket beside the road. One night it had rained and they had to scramble to get in the car before they were soaked. Another night they had spotted a shack, not quite tumbledown, and she thought it would be a good place to bed down for the night. However, when they got to the door, there was a dead snake about 3 feet long laying right in front of the door. She couldn't persuade the kids to step over it. To tell the truth, she wasn't crazy about it herself.

A deep despair had overtaken her and she didn't even look up as an old battered pickup truck came from the other way and slowed down. The driver eased on past and went on his way.

She managed to pull herself out of the blue funk she was in and got out of the car. They had passed a farm about a quarter of a mile back. She had never asked for help before and wouldn't even now if it wasn't for Joey and Ruthie. How could she let them go to bed with nothing but a slice of bread in their stomachs? Maybe the farmer would let her do some work for something to eat. Maybe they would even let them sleep in the barn tonight. Hopefully, there wouldn't be other transients sleeping there, too. As she helped Ruthie out of the car, Joey said, in a small voice, "What are we going to do, Mom?"

"Please don't ask me that question, son. I don't rightly know what we're going to do, and it upsets me to have you ask," she replied. "I think we are going to walk back down to that farm and see if we can get some help." Joey was a good boy who tried real hard not to upset his Mom, but he was after all, just an 8-year-old boy, tuned in to his mother's emotions. He knew that times were hard and he missed his Dad who had been gone ever so long. Sometimes he could hear his Mom crying at night so he knew she missed him, too. He tried to take care of Ruthie for her and helped her whenever he could. They had had to leave Dutch, their collie with a neighbor and he missed the dog, too.

Ruthie, in a whiny voice said, "Mama, I don't want to walk. Will you carry me?" Emily answered her in explicit tones, " I don't want to walk, either, Ruthie, will you carry me?" Ruthie heaved a big sigh and gave up the quest. It was late afternoon and they were thirsty and hungry.

When they reached the farmhouse, there was an old truck parked up by the back door. It just barely rang a bell in Emily's mind. Then it dawned on her that it was the truck that had slowed down to pass them. She hadn't noticed who was driving. She stepped up on the porch and knocked on the door while the children hung back and held hands. When no one responded, she knocked

Emily

BY

CARLEEN SHEA

RoseDog Books

PITTSBURGH, PENNSYLVANIA 15222

For more information or to order additional books, please contact:
RoseDog Books
701 Smithfield Street
Third Floor
Pittsburgh, Pennsylvania 15222
U.S.A.
1-800-834-1803
www.rosedogbookstore.com

louder. She looked through the screen door and could see a sack of groceries sitting on the cupboard. The thought crossed her mind that if she took the groceries and hurried back to the car, they could eat before anyone missed them. The foolishness of that thought hit her then and she decided she would get farther by asking for something to eat. It wouldn't do her kids any good if she landed in jail for stealing food.

She went around to the front door with Joey and Ruthie tagging along behind her, but she couldn't see any signs of life there either. Maybe whoever lived here was in the barn but it was a little scary to think of going out there to look. There was a chicken coop with a few chickens wandering around freely and she could see a garden quite close to one side of the house. They went back to the back door and sat down on the steps to wait. Certainly there was someone around somewhere. She was sure that was the truck she had seen on the road. With nothing else to occupy her mind, she began to observe her surroundings more closely. There was a fresh straw stack out in the barnyard, which meant that wheat or oats had just been harvested. A windmill stood out by the barnyard fence with a trough leading through the fence into a water tank for the stock. The well platform sported a `pump which could be operated by hand in case the wind didn't blow. There were no vanes missing from the wheel. The garden had looked clean so whoever lived here must take pretty good care of things. The house and barn both could stand a coat of paint but who had money these days to spend on paint? Off to the side of the barn was an orchard. She thought there were apple trees and maybe even peach trees. There was a big, old oak tree out by the driveway with a rope swing hanging down from a bottom limb, which must have been 20 feet from the ground. She had had such a swing in her life but she doubted that her kids would even know what to do with one.

Forty-five minutes later, a middle aged man and a younger man came out of the barn door. They were both wearing bib overalls with long sleeved plaid shirts. The younger man was a bit taller than the other and they both had dark hair, though the older man's hair was peppered with gray. Each carried a pail of milk in each hand. They went to the windmill where they put a milk strainer on top of a milk can and poured the milk in. Putting the cover on the can they lifted it into a tub of cold well water. After the strainer and pails were washed, upended on a bench, and covered with a cloth, they turned toward the house. They both noticed the group sitting on the steps at the same time.

"Well, Donald, looks like we got company," the older man said, "I told you they'd be visitin' us, didn't I?"

"You sure did, Pop, but where's the man? I didn't even see him at the car when we went by." Donald was puzzled. Wasn't there supposed to be a man with this woman and kids? Was he hanging back out of sight waiting to steal something from them? He and Pop had been pretty generous with all these people down on their luck but they didn't like to have things stolen from them. And they had not had any female visitors without a man before today.

The older man stepped forward and held out his hand. "My name's Vern Morrison and this here's my son, Donald. My wife, Vera, isn't here right now.

Her folks are both sick up in West Virginia. Her brother came down to get her to help take care of them. Don't know how long it's goin' to take to get them well, but Donald and me decided that we'd better learn to batch it. That your car down there beside the road? What's the matter with it?"

Donald, who wasn't quite as wordy as his father, stepped forward then and held his hand out to Emily. "We saw you earlier, sitting beside the road. See you had a flat tire. Maybe we can help you fix it."

Emily stood up then and extended her hand toward the men. "My name is Emily Jones and these are my children Joey and Ruthie. We're trying to get to Redhouse, Virginia, where my sister lives. There's something wrong with the car besides a flat tire. It just quit out here."

Donald spoke up, "Where's your man?"

There was a long moment of silence while the two men looked at everything in view as though they had never seen it before and were examining it minutely so they could make a major purchase. The two kids had their eyes riveted on the men and before Emily could speak, Joey said in a clear, manly voice, "He went to California to look for work. He was going to send for us but we never heard from him. We think something bad has happened to him, 'cause he would never leave us this long if he was all right." Emily almost went into shock at this statement. She had never discussed the possibility of something bad happening to Harlan with the children. She surmised that she would have to start looking at Joey with different eyes. And again, before Emily could speak, Ruthie said, "We're hungry. We haven't had anything to eat since this morning." Emily noticed that the little girl had dropped the whiny voice and was just stating facts as clearly as she knew how. Maybe, Emily thought, I'm going to have to start looking at both of them in a different way.

Emily quickly added her two cents worth. "We don't mind doing some work to pay for some food, but Ruthie's right. We are powerful hungry."

"What can you do as far as work is concerned?" asked Vern.

Emily replied, "I can cook and clean and weed your garden. I can play the organ a little bit."

Joey piped up, "I can pump some water for you and feed your cows."

Ruthie said, "I can go out and pick up the swing board and put it in the swing."

Emily looked at her daughter in astonishment. She did know what to do with a swing, after all. She kept silent, but was thinking that maybe she had been underestimating her children.

The men both burst into laughter. Donald said, "Well we might have to think on the organ thing for a bit seein' as how we don't have one, but a meal cooked by somebody besides Pop would be mighty tasty."

Vern told her, "Why don't you go in and see what we have to do your cookin' with and Donald and me will take the tractor down and pull your car up into the yard where we can look at it better. The boy here can come with us. The cows are all taken care of for the night. But don't worry, mornin's comin' and they'll need to be fed and watered again." Turning to Ruthie, he said, "That there swing board has been on the ground for a long time. I been meanin' to pick it up but just never got around to it. You better test that swing 'cause nobody has used it since Donald was a little tad and I don't know if it still works or not." The three 'men' left on the tractor with Donald driving and Joey on the seat in front of him with his hands on the steering wheel while Vern stood on a platform behind the seat.

Ruthie headed for the swing and Emily went into the kitchen. First she looked in the sack of groceries on the shelf by the icebox. There was sugar, flour, a loaf of bread, and a ring of bologna. Her mouth watered even as she looked at it. Did she need to ask if she could use it or not? The icebox yielded a large dish of yellow string beans from the garden and a gallon crock of fresh milk. Oh, would the kids ever love that! She decided quickly that she would cook the string beans and fry some of the bologna. The store-bought bread would do for tonight but in the morning she would make some biscuits. She had also discovered some coffee beans and a coffee pot, so that would round out their supper in fine fettle.

There was a shed partly sunk into the ground out in the side yard and even as she was looking at it, Donald came around the corner of the house and disappeared into it. "Aha!" she thought, "it's a root cellar." When he came in he was carrying a glass jar of peaches.

The kid's eyes were as big as silver dollars as they sat down to this sumptuous repast. When the meal was almost finished, Vern settled back and cleared his throat. "I guess I lied to you a little bit. My wife is not in West Virginia. Her name was Flora and she died last fall about Thanksgivin' time. Me and Donald been batchin' it all right but it was because we had to. These peaches reminded me that she would be kind of ashamed of me for lyin'. It's gonna be another new experience for us to try to can our garden and orchard stuff. We found her canning book and we been reading up on it some but it ain't gonna be easy."

The next morning she found some eggs in the icebox and Donald brought a piece of fatback in from the root cellar. He explained that it was built over a small stream at the back of the yard and the stream kept food pretty cold. Also, that was where his mother had kept her canned goods. And they had a barrel of coffee beans out there, too. The reason they didn't keep much food in the icebox was so they wouldn't have to buy ice in town.

She proceeded to make biscuits and coffee to go with the eggs and fatback and when the men came in for breakfast, the house smelled delicious. The talk turned to the future of her automobile. According to Donald, there didn't seem to be much hope. He said he would try but he would have to fashion some parts out of the materials he could find around the place.

It seemed that they were involved in cultivating the corn and needed to keep at it. She told him that her sister and husband were not really expecting them at any special time so she didn't have to worry about that.

As Donald and Vern left for the field, they both acted rather embarrassed and stammered all around the issue. What have I done wrong? She wondered. But, no, all they wanted to tell her was that breakfast had been mighty good.

Chapter 2

EMILY 'PLAYS THE ORGAN' FOR HER SUPPER

After the kitchen was cleaned up, she went out to take a look at the root cellar and was amazed at the supplies inside. She noted how many empty quart jars there were waiting to be filled. Would Donald and Vern ever be able to get it done? She then wandered out to the garden. Lifting up the bean leaves, she was amazed once again. These vines were loaded and ready to be picked and canned; a few more days and they would be wasted. She scouted around the basement and found a bushel basket. She also found Flora's canning equipment in a cupboard in the basement all clean and covered with a cloth.

Joey had gone to the field with the men to fulfill his part of the bargain supposedly, but she thought that he just needed the companionship of the male gender. Ruthie was sitting in the swing and slowly finding out how to pump the swing up in the air. Emily summoned her and said, " I'm going to pick the string beans and can them. Could I get you to help me?" Ruthie jumped down from the swing and told her mother, "You know, Mama, that picking up the swing board really wasn't much of a job. Maybe if I help you can the beans, Vern and Donald will know I'm not really such a little girl." Emily laughed harder than she had laughed in a year.

She and the little girl both worked hard at picking the string beans and by 10:00 the basket was full to overflowing. She put a stick in the ground to mark where they had left off picking and they set up a work station on the back porch to snap the beans and wash them. At noon when she went in to see what she could get for lunch, they had the beans all ready for the canning process. Donald and Vern, on seeing what she had done, set right off for the root cellar to bring Flora's glass jars in for her. "Hey, Pop," Donald said, "if this just ain't the

Doggies. I didn't know she was goin' to do this." Vern replied, "Well, son, maybe you hadn't ought to be too eager to get that car fixed."

The tomatoes came right on top of the beans and the cucumbers came on top of the tomatoes and the sweet corn came after that. Nothing was said about the Jones family leaving and it seemed like there would never be a break in the harvesting so Emily figured they would let her know when she and the kids were not welcome any more. With everything that was put in cans for winter, she thought she could see a little more relief in Donald's face. The men, who by now included Joey, took care of the potato harvest. Just when Emily thought she was done canning, Vern came to the house with a bushel of peaches from the orchard.

Emily was aware that Donald had not even looked at her car, but she had been lulled by all of the domesticity in which she had been indulging herself. She had been feeding the chickens regularly and they had rewarded her with increasing quantities of eggs. She and the kids had been here for 3 months now and had been eating healthy food regularly and the kids had all the milk they could drink. With two good men for role models, Joey was indeed becoming a man. She was becoming edgy about leaving. She didn't want to overstay her welcome but life had become so comfortable that she didn't want to leave. Her uneasiness about the situation was solved one night in August when Vern said that he and Donald wanted to have a talk with her after the kids went to bed. Almost sick to her stomach with nerves because she thought they were going to tell her to leave she cleaned up the supper mess under their watchful eyes. Donald had chosen this night to help her as he sometimes did. She kept putzing around the kitchen with busy work when Donald took her by the arm and put the dishcloth on the rack and said, "Enough, Emily, come in the living room now so we can talk." With a sigh and a grim look on her face, she followed him into the room.

Vern said, "Now, Emmy, ain't no use in looking like you got a death sentence. It ain't that bad!" She sat in the rocker by the window and the two men sat on the couch. Vern said, "I'm gonna start and then Donald is gonna have his say and then you'll get a chance to have yours." She thought of all the hours of work she had put in here and how she had enjoyed it. She thought of all the positive effects there had been for each one of them. She hoped that she wouldn't cry.

Vern started: "We didn't have any idea that day we saw the three of you sittin' on the front porch what we was in for. Our first thought was to help you get your car started and on the way to wherever you were goin'. But you and the kids wormed your way into our lives and I don't know how we would have managed this first year without Flora if you hadn't come along. We were gonna wing it the best we could with cannin' and everything but I'm not sure we would have been anything like successful. The upshot of this talk is that we want you to stay forever and the only way we can see to do that is for one of us to marry you."

Donald picked up the conversation then: "Pop, I told you not to say that. You're not gonna get the chance. I'm the one that's gonna marry her." He looked at Emily then and smiled: "I told him I never did want a stepmother. Mom would have been the one to want you to be my sister. She would have loved you. She would have loved the kids, too." He got up quickly and went to the kitchen. His voice had started to quaver and she saw some moisture around his eyes. But he came right back in with a glass of water and handed it to her.

Emily said, "I'm very touched. You have both been so good to us, but you have to remember that I have a husband somewhere. And even if something has happened to him I can't commit to anyone until I know for sure. He was a good man and I am positive that if he were alive I would have heard from him sometime in the last year. Still, I am legally married until proven otherwise."

Donald picked up the conversation: "I don't know how, Emily, but I swear, I will try to find out where he is for you. Will you stay with us?" And then, she did start crying. She was remembering how desperate she was that day when her car quit down the road and how these two beautiful men had saved her sanity, her life, and her children's lives.

Donald continued: "It's almost time for school to start. Have the kids ever been to school? Joey says he can write his name but they both need to be in school. I can get the old pony cart out and spruce it up and Joey can learn to drive Topsy. She is so old, she could never run away. Or maybe they could just learn to ride her bareback. Neither one is heavy enough but what they could ride double."

Vern, who had been thoughtfully pondering his next argument, spoke up, "If'n the township can't afford to hire a teacher this year, we can set up a school right here in the kitchen. Emmy, you're pretty well spoken. You must have some education. Donald learned a good deal of his sums here at this old kitchen table with his Mama sitting in as teacher. And he's pretty good at sums; he could probably help you.

She had written to her sister in Redhouse a week or so after she arrived in Perryville and told her what had happened. A letter came back by return mail and Jane had said she was worried about them, but underneath Emily could hear a sigh of relief.

Chapter 3

DAGGETT BROWN

It was Thanksgiving time again and there was a bit of melancholy in the air as the men remembered their wife and mother. Emily had learned that Flora had cut herself on the hand two weeks before and infection had settled in. Vern took her into town to old Doc Pritchard but blood poisoning had started and she had red streaks up her arm to her elbow. Medicine was more or less still in a primitive state and she hung on for another week and died two days before the holiday.

Overlaying the melancholy was an air of festivity. Earlier in the week Vern had received a letter from his brother-in-law who lived about 40 miles away near Gulchy Gap. He was on his way right now to spend Thanksgiving with the Morrisons. Vern explained that they had not heard from him since last spring and even though he was sort of a strange one, he would be made welcome. His name was Dag Brown and Vern suspected that he was lonesome and they had urged him to come more often.. Emily started making plans to entertain a guest and planning dinner. She would kill a couple of the old roosters that were getting too fat. What did they need of more than 1 or 2 roosters, anyway? It was the day before and she had been keeping an eye out for a car to come down the road. She was standing at the kitchen sink cleaning vegetables when her eye caught a movement out in the woods. As she watched a small man on a mule materialized and came out on the trail into the lane behind the barn. He was coming alongside the barn when Donald appeared at the barn door and spotted him. He yelled, "Pop! Pop! Uncle Dag's here." and he started running toward the mule that had stopped dead in its tracks at all the racket.

"Well, Dang it, boy, ya scared Old Prancer here, most out of her wits. I thought she was gonna run away." As far as Emily had seen, Old Prancer wasn't geared up to take another step. Uncle Dag dismounted the mule and Emily could see him a lot better. He was about 5 foot 6 inches and had a gray beard about 6 inches long. He wore old bib overalls with an awkward patch on one knee and a plaid flannel shirt that was faded and worn. On his head was an old straw hat that had seen better days. Try as she might, Emily could not see any baggage that would indicate a few days stay. "Oh, well!" she thought, "Maybe what you see is what you get." And, anyway, the irascible old man hadn't seemed to dampen Donald's enthusiasm. He took Old Prancer's reins in hand to put him in the barn, but Old Prancer wasn't buying into that idea, either. When Uncle Dag saw the ensuing tug-of-war, he took the reins back and with a word or two, the mule followed him into the barn with a docile demeanor.

Presently the three men approached the house and Emily could see that this was not really an old man. He was probably of the same vintage as Vern. Both of the Morison's were giving him the glad hand and seemed happy to see him. Just before they came in the door, Emily remembered Vern's remark about Dag being sort of a strange one. Donald did the introductions and Uncle Dag seemed to be scrutinizing Emily something beyond normal. Finally, he removed his hat and said, "Howdy, girl, pleased to meetcha! Vern here didn't tell me he had other company. You Donald's girl?"

Just then Joey and Ruthie came clamoring down the stairs. Emily said, "No, sir, me and my kids are just staying here until Donald can get my car running again. So we try to help out as much as we can." Vern proudly informed Dag that she had been here 3 months and had filled every one of Flora's 400 quart canning jars with produce from the garden and orchard and had helped out at butchering time, too.

Dag reared back and fixed a pointed look on Vern and said, "You boys was worried about Flora's cannin', wasn't you?" Vern replied that they were worried about a lot of things that Flora had contributed to the household. Then he added, "This Emily gal has been worth her weight in gold."

Joey and Ruthie who had been hanging back so as not to interrupt the conversation, came forward now and introduced themselves to Uncle Dag. Joey offered his hand just as he had seen the men do. Ruthie followed suit and did the same.

Emily's two old roosters were the stars of the day. She had cooked them until they were tender and made mashed potatoes, biscuits and gravy and cornbread dressing. For dessert she had made two apple pies and served them with thick cream to pour over them. The meal was silent for the most part. These people took their eating seriously, especially when there was a good meal on the table. Uncle Dag chewed slowly and savored every bite, but what Emily noticed most of all was that he was watching her. Three times she had glanced up and found herself pinned to the wall with his eagle-eye stare.

There was an extra guest at the table, also. A hobo who called himself Merritt had shown up at the door about mid-morning and said he was hungry. Vern had taken him out to the windmill and shown him where he could wash up, given him some clean clothes to wear while they ran a load of clothes in Flora's washing machine. Said washing machine had a wooden tub with an agitator that moved by power provided by a foot pedal on the outside of the machine. The wringer had a hand crank, so with Merritt sitting on a stool beside the washer and providing foot power, his clothes were soon hanging on the clothesline to dry. Vern had always been mindful of the workload of a farmer's wife and tried to provide Flora with the best possible tools to work with. Vern explained to Emily that he always liked to share their bounty with the less fortunate. And the less fortunate were not hard to come by these days.

After dinner, the men got up from the table and to Emily's surprise, Uncle Dag waited until the rest of them had gone into the sitting room, and he said, "Well, now, Emmy-girl, I'm a gonna help you clean up here so you can come in and sit down with us." She might have expected Donald to help or even Vern but Uncle Dag? The uneasy feeling that he had been giving her dissipated once they started washing the dishes. It was like somebody had suddenly vaccinated him with a phonograph needle. He was telling her about his farm, his mule, and his trip to Perryville, almost non-stop. He was still looking at her with his piercing gray eyes, but it no longer bothered her after they had a few laughs. She told him about Harlan setting off for California and how they hadn't heard from him in almost two years. His reply was to shake his head and say, "Tsk-tsk!" When they were almost done with the clean up, he asked, "You plan on staying here?" She thought for a minute before she answered, "I didn't plan on staying here at all, and I guess if they say they don't want me here any more, I will try to get to my sister's in Virginia." He stepped squarely in front of her then, and putting his hands on her shoulders, he said, "Don't you go movin' on to Virginny, girl. Tain't likely they'll be askin you to leave, but if they should, you just get word to me and I'll come and get you and your children. I got a wagon and Old Prancer can still pull it if I coax her just right. Tears started coming to her eyes and she reached out and patted Uncle Dag on the cheek.

In the sitting room, Donald had a deck of cards out and was teaching Joey, Ruthie, and Merritt how to play Loo, a game in which they could all participate. When dark began to settle in, Vern said, "Donald, why don't you take Merritt out to the barn and show him where he can bunk down for the night?" Merritt thanked all of them for his day and his meal and produced his own blanket from his backpack. The next morning when the men went out to milk the cows, he was gone with only a dent in the haymow to remind the Morrisons that he had ever been there.

Chapter 4

DAG'S WORDS OF WISDOM

Dag had more things to say to each of the family but they were things he had to say in private. Vern knew him well enough that he saw an agenda in Dag's mind but hadn't figured out yet what it was. It was going on into the third day and Dag hadn't said a word about going home. It was driving Vern crazy. It wasn't that Dag wasn't welcome; it just wasn't like him. He always had to hurry home and take care of things there. He had offered to let the kids ride Old Prancer yesterday and they had gone back down the lane with him leading and cajoling the mule. When they got as far as Old Prancer would go, he said, "Guess we all need to set and rest a spell." He started out by asking if they liked it here. Joey said, "Yeah, and Vern and Donald let me help them. Donald says this summer he is going to teach me to drive the tractor and milk the cows. I already pump water when the wind doesn't blow. And he says I can help with the haying. I did some last summer but I am 3 inches taller now and a lot stronger." Dag asked, "You like Donald pretty well?" Ruthie spoke up then: "Oh, yeah! And we like Vern, too. But we miss our daddy. I wish we knew what happened to him." Dag asked how they knew that something had happened to him. Joey said, "He was a good dad and he wouldn't just leave us if he was all right." Dag thought for a minute about what to say- then: "Bad things happen to good people sometimes. We just have to keep puttin' one foot in front of the other and carryin' on." He turned to Ruthie and said, "You do a mighty fine job on that rope swing, Little Missy. She liked it when he called her Little Missy but she pursed her mouth up all prim and proper and said, " I do a whole lot more than that, Uncle Dag. Mama says that was just busy work that Vern gave me to do because he thought I was too little. I helped Mama with the canning, and I set the table before meals all the time. Mama says she is going to teach me how to sew so I can help patch our clothes. Maybe next time you come I can put a better patch on your overalls." Not knowing exactly what to say, Dag examined the patch he had put on his knee closely and did, indeed, find it wanting. He started to rise to his feet when Joey, catching him unawares, said, "Did something bad happen to you, Uncle Dag?" Dag looked back down the lane while he tried to think of what he wanted to say. Finally he said, "Reckon so!"

This morning, Donald had said that he was going to drive into town to get some supplies they were getting short on and Dag had informed him that he also wanted to go to town. Vern, sensing that Dag wanted this trip to be his and Donald's, begged off by saying he had a couple of jobs to do this afternoon. It was about 5 miles into town and Donald could have walked it pretty easy but not if he had to carry supplies. The days were past when he just wanted to go to town for entertainment. They got out on the road and Donald said, "When you gonna get yourself a truck, Uncle Dag?" "Well, now," Dag replied, "I don't rightly see where I need one. Might make Old Prancer feel useless and she's the best friend I got." He made the funny little cackle that he called a laugh. A few silent seconds passed and then Dag asked, "What you planning' to do about Emmy?"

Donald sobered up in a hurry and said, "Now, Dag, why you want to hit me over the head with a 2x4 like that? You know what her story is. She's not even free until she knows what happened to her husband. And if she never finds out it will be 7 years before he can be declared dead." Dag waited a few minutes and he noticed they were approaching town and he'd better have his say pretty quick. "Shuckins, Donald, you 'n me both knows that he ain't comin' back. These is bad times. I see the lay of the land the way you look at her. Don't you let that little gal slip through your fingers." Donald asked him, "Just what would you have me do?" Dag got a sly look on his face and said, "Once you get her in bed with you, she ain't gonna talk about leavin'."

After supper was over and the chores done, Dag said to Vern, "Let's take a walk back down the lane, I saw something there I want to ask you about." When they were a distance from the house, Vern inquired as to what Dag wanted to ask him about. The conversation went thus:

Dag: "Shuckins, ain't nothing' out here I want to know about. I wanted to tell you sumpthin'"

Vern: "Well, shoot!"

Dag: "I got a feelin' about this here Emmy"

Vern: "A feelin'? You ain't getting' funny pants in your old age, are ya?"

Dag: (with his cackle laugh) "Wish I was, but, no, I ain't. The first minute I seen her, I felt like there was a connection, like I knew her in another life, if such a thing is possible. Ya know, I never said much about my Maybelle but when Henrietta took her and went away- just disappeared- it dang near killed me. Twice I almost called her Maybelle. Do you know anything about her parents?"

Vern:" No, but I don't suppose there's any reason I can't get into a conversation with her about it."

Dag: "How old is she, do you know?"

Vern: "I think she said she is thirty years old next September"

Dag: "Well, Henrietta took off with Maybelle when she was two years old and that was in '04. She'd be just about the right age. Her hair is a little darker but that could be expected. She's got the same gray eyes as I got."

Vern: "Where'd she take off to, anyway?"

Dag: " She snuck out the window and went off with that drummer fellow that was goin' through town. I didn't care about her, but why she had to take my little girl I never could figger out. I could have taken care of her and I don't think Henrietta cared that much about her."

Vern kept his silence. He had known how hard it was for Dag to lose his daughter, but he really thought it was stretching it a bit to believe that a girl who had fallen into their lives (literally) could be the one he wanted her to be.

Dag spoke up: "I told Donald he'd better get her into his bed"

Vern: (angrily) "How could you do that? If she's who you think, then she's Donald's cousin. We can't have any mixin' of the blood like that."

Dag: "You listen to me, Vern. I'm only goin to say this once. You know as well as I do where Donald come from, and there'll be no mixin' of the blood. Henrietta was your sister. Does Donald know anything about his blood?"

Vern could only stare at Dag. He had never had any idea that Dag knew.

Chapter 5

CHRISTMAS PRESENTS

Dag left right after breakfast the next morning with an old set of saddlebags full of food for the trip home. Vern had found them in the old harness room in the barn and cleaned them up. Emily had packed them with food. She laughed as she watched him go back down the lane and disappear into the woods. "How long will it take him to get home, Donald," she asked. "Well," he said, given Prancer's fondness for running away, probably a week." They both laughed heartily and Donald prepared to go to the barn where Vern had been working in the woodshop. The two of them had been working on Christmas presents for the children. Vern was carving a wooden rifle for Joey and making a doll cradle for Ruthie. Emily was making Ruthie a cloth doll and she was sewing shirts for the three men, including Joey. She had discovered a cache of new cloth in the attic that Flora must have put there. She had also had her eye on the New Home Treadle Sewing Machine in the parlor. She had never used one but had looked this one over real good and thought she could work it with a little practice. By now she thought she knew Flora well enough that the woman would not mind her using it.

Donald had uncovered a saddle he had used as a young man and was working saddle soap into it to soften the leather and make it shine. He sort of thought that maybe he would make a new swing board, put some fancy carving on it, and varnish it for Ruthie. They were both stumped on what they could give Emily for Christmas. Suddenly, Donald said, "Hey Pop, do you think she knows how to sew?" Vern answered, "She's right smart. I'd bet my last dollar that she does. Are ya thinkin' about your mama's box of cloth in the attic?" That afternoon, they made a visit to the attic and found Flora's box and there right on top was a pretty piece of blue and white dimity. Vern said, " I wonder if your mama was goin' to make herself a dress out of this before she died." and Donald nodded his head ever so slightly in agreement.

They all had their secrets. Even Joey and Ruthie had picked a kitten out of the new litter of barn cats to give their mother for a present. Ruthie had a red ribbon that she had been hoarding since they had left Wolf Creek. They made plans to tie the ribbon around the kitten's neck and put it under the Christmas tree. Donald had already said that they would put up a tree and he knew where the ornaments were to decorate it. Everybody was excited but Emily thought that something was lacking. One morning when she woke up it struck her what it was. There was nothing to put under the tree for Uncle Dag. True, he had given no indication that he would be there for Christmas, nor had he ever been, but it wouldn't hurt anything to have a gift for him. And besides she had liked the old man since the day he helped her clean up in the kitchen and so generously offered to take them into his home. She hustled through her morning chores and went up to the attic. Pulling the box of cloth out of its place she opened it up. But something was wrong. Then she knew what it was. The pretty piece of blue and white dimity that she liked so well and intended to ask Vern about after Christmas was gone. She went through the whole box thinking that maybe she had put it back underneath the other pieces. No, it just wasn't there. Where could it be? If Donald had a girl friend, maybe he would have given it to her. But she was fairly sure he didn't have a girl friend. Anyway, that wouldn't be an appropriate gift for a girl friend. A bit downcast, she went back downstairs with a piece of plaid cloth to make a shirt for Uncle Dag.

When Donald came in for supper that night, he had sort of a silly grin on his face. Emily knew that you weren't supposed to ask questions or snoop at Christmas time. She couldn't help but wonder. She arose from her chair and went to the sink where she had just hung a clean blue and white towel- the blue and white cloth! Suddenly she knew what Donald's silly grin was about. She was going to get the piece of cloth for Christmas to make herself a new dress. She looked at Donald's handsome face and thought about how kind he had been to them. No, it would not be too much of a hardship to fall in love with Donald. Well, one thing was for sure. She was either going to have to forget that she had thought of this or gear herself up to be surprised. It would never do to let them know that she had found out.

Chapter 6

The Christmas Tree

Almost every week a transient would stop outside and ask for something to eat. It wasn't long before Emily and the kids knew the drill. Vern or Donald would take him out to the windmill to clean up, provide him with temporary clothes while the man would sit on the stool beside the washing machine and provide foot power to wash his own clothes. The next morning with a full belly and a good night's sleep, he would leave. Every time Emily saw a lone figure walking on the road, she would scrutinize him carefully for signs that he might be Harlan. Once she had observed Joey doing the same thing. There weren't as many of the transients in this part of the country because most of them were going from the Midwest to California.

A couple of days before Christmas there was a moderate snowfall, making everything beautiful. Everyone was in good spirits and Donald had rummaged around in the attic until he found a box of his old clothes that his mother had placed behind a bunch of other boxes. He came downstairs with two small coats that he could barely remember, a triumphant smile on his face. He had hitched Topsy to the sleigh and they all boarded and headed for the woods to look for just the right tree. There were jingle bells on Topsy's harness to add to the gala event. It took them an hour just to find the right one. Every one they looked at was either too tall, too short, crooked trunk, or lop-sided. When they finally agreed on one, they all watched breathlessly while Donald chopped it down and tied it across the back of the sleigh.

Back at the house, Emily had a big pan of cocoa on the back of the cook stove. While she and Ruthie were getting it ready, the 'men' went out to the workshop where Vern and Donald fashioned a base for the tree. In a few minutes they came in with the tree and placed it in the parlor. After the cocoa, they got down to the serious business of placing the tree and decorating it with a box of ornaments, some of them homemade, that Vern had brought from the attic. Since the new thing called electricity was a few years away from the rural areas yet, the only option they had for lights on the tree was candlepower and Vern didn't want to risk a fire in the house. But that was all right. The kids had never even had much of a tree let alone lights.

They had not heard from Uncle Dag, but that was not unusual. His visit was always at Thanksgiving time. The kids went to bed on Christmas Eve full of plans. They had sneaked the kitten up to Joey's bedroom and, in the morning, he would tie the ribbon around Tessy's neck, put her in a box, and sneak downstairs early to put her under the tree. All plans went as expected and Ruthie swore that she heard Santa Claus on the roof in the night. Joey went back upstairs and waited for the household to wake up. About half an hour later he began to hear the occupants stirring and he waited behind the door until his mother and Ruthie went down. Vern and Donald were already in the kitchen. There was much to-do about all the presents, but none of the adults had expected anything so their presents were a real bonus. Emily was over-joyed at the piece of yard goods for a new dress and nobody had the slightest inkling that she had known about it beforehand. The 'men' were delighted with their new shirts, but could hardly understand why there was something there for Uncle Dag. He never came at Christmas time. Then Ruthie remembered the box around behind the tree, but it was empty. She and Joey looked in the bedrooms and the kitchen. They even looked out the windows to see if Tessy had escaped and was back outdoors. With disappointed faces they told their mother that they had a present for her but they had to find it. Suddenly they heard a loud "MEOW" from the tree and there, almost to the top was a pair of green eyes looking out through the branches. Donald immediately rescued her and they all had a good laugh, while Emily admired her unexpected Christmas present.

Chapter 7

UNCLE DAG RETURNS

There was to be another good chicken dinner as the chickens were really thriving now and last summer's crop of baby chicks had been a 'bumper' crop. They were almost ready to sit down at the table and there had been no unexpected visitors for the meal, when they heard a jingle of harness bells. Running to the door, who should they see but Uncle Dag coming in from the road with Old Prancer hooked up to a sleigh. Not only was she hooked up to it; she was prancing along right smart. Dag told them that he figured it would liven Prancer up to have the harness bells jingling, and sure enough, it had only taken them nine hours to get here. Donald hoped privately that Old Prancer would not go out to the barn and meet her demise after this lively journey. In the seat beside him was a burlap bag with something bulky in it. He took it in the kitchen and there was much oohing and ahing when he disclosed that it was a large ham from his smokehouse.

Ruthie came running out of the parlor with Uncle Dag's present in her hands, and when he opened it up, he was so pleased with his new shirt that he couldn't quit grinning. Then, as though it was something he had completely forgotten, he threw his hands up in the air and let out a joyful whoop. He ran back out to the sleigh and retrieved another burlap bag from the boot of the sleigh. In it was a pair of ice skates for Joey that had to be something from Dag's childhood. For Ruthie, there was a doll with a dress made of a flowered print that Uncle Dag explained had been his little girl's dolly when she lived with him. They were all familiar with the story of Uncle Dag's little Maybelle, and Emily was glad that he could talk about it now as he hadn't been able to do so for many years. For Emily there was a dress that had been Henrietta's and it was made of the same flowered print as the doll dress. He had brought some woodworking tools for the men and Donald told her later that they were out of Dag's own workshop. Emily thought, "What good men these are!"

Dinner was almost over and it had been eaten like most of their meals, in silence, when Emily glanced over at Ruthie's chair where 'Dolly' sat propped up behind her new Mama. Something clicked in her mind, and she arose and ran upstairs. Digging down into a chest at the foot of the bed, she came up with a small dress made of the same flowered print as the dolly dress and Henrietta's dress that Dag had given her. Carrying it out in front of her, she said, "My mother and father who raised me were not really my parents. They told me that I was left on their doorstep when I was about 2 years old. They had never been able to have any children until after I came to live with them, so they never reported me to authorities. It was in April 1904, and they didn't know my birthday so they gave me the birthday of April 2 and kept me for their own. Mother said I had on this little dress." She held the dress up and everybody just stared at it. She picked up the doll and held it next to the child's dress. Dag hung his head and tried to keep the secret that he was wiping tears out of his eyes. When he could speak, he said quietly, " I knew it! I just knew it the first time I saw you, Emmy-girl, that there was something' 'portant about you. That's why I offered to take you home with me. Henrietta made those clothes just afore she left; one for her, one for Maybelle, and a dolly dress for 'Doris'. That's what Maybelle called her dolly. She left in such a hurry that she didn't even take all her things." Donald showed a bit of surprise at the news that Uncle Dag had tried to lure Emily away from them.

Chapter 8

DONALD

Donald was moping. He was very quiet and spent a lot of time out in the barn. Uncle Dag had been there a week and he was beyond doubt taking up every minute of Emily's time that he possibly could. Donald thought he might even be trying to get her to go home with him. The truth of the matter was that Dag could hardly get enough of Emily and the kids. After all those years of wondering what had happened to her, here she was right where he could touch her and talk to her any time he wanted to. And she was likewise anxious to talk to him about her past. She still called him Uncle Dag but that didn't bother him. She had found a box of dressmaker's patterns in the attic and when the everyday chores were done she would sit in the parlor and sew on her new dress. Uncle Dag would sit with her just talking and talking and telling her stories about the family. She loved the old man more and more.

Vern left them more or less alone to get acquainted, but he had begun to notice that something was not setting well with Donald. He asked Donald at the supper table to come out to the barn and help him move something. They had moved a few things in the harness room when Donald said, "When is he goin' home?"

Vern replied, "Well, now, Donald, Dag has passed a whole lot of years wonderin' where his little daughter went. We can cut him a little slack, can't we?"

Donald said, "This has spoiled everything for me. I wanted to marry her and now I can't."

Vern didn't understand at first and then recognition hit him. He felt like somebody had given him a sucker punch in the belly, but he knew the time had come to tell Donald a few facts. He busied himself building up a fire in the small heating stove in the room and pulled up a couple of wooden boxes to sit on and started talking. He said, "Just listen until I am through because this isn't easy for me to tell you." Donald agreed with a nod of his head. Vern started: "First of all, you've been about the best son a man could have. I've always been proud of you and your mother was, too. I knew Flora all my life but her folks were a little more upscale than mine. We was just farmers living out here on this old farm that had been in our family for a hundred years. Her family owned a dry goods store in town and she was the apple of her daddy's eye. Then a new banker came to town and he had a son who was just a bit on the wild side. He took Flora's eye and he started courting' her, at least that's what everybody thought he was doin'. Very suddenly the banker got a job in Chicago and they were moving. A couple of weeks later, I went into the dry goods store for sump thin' and Flora's Pa wanted me to come into the backroom with him. I didn't have any idea what was comin'. He got right to the point. Flora was in the family way and he had made a list of all the eligible young men in town that would be suitable for his daughter to marry. I have to say that it made me proud that I was # 1 on the list." Vern had sort of a little sideways grin on his face, but Donald looked like someone had pole-axed him and he was looking at Vern as though he was some kind of an alien. Vern continued: " I tried to figure out some way to tell you so it wouldn't be such a shock, but I don't think I managed to do it. I might just as well finish my story. I told her father that I couldn't promise anything until I had talked to her. I could probably count the number of times I had talked to her on the fingers of one hand. So I got dressed up in my Sunday best and went to call on her. She knew what the gist of the meeting was and we sat down in the parlor. I told her I had talked with her father. She sat there with her eyes downcast and I thought she was the most beautiful thing I had ever seen. When I asked her to marry me, she started cryin' and asked me if I knew about the baby because she wouldn't try to deceive me. I said I knew and that I would try to be the best husband and father that I could possibly be. I had no idea what to do with a cryin' woman but I guess I let my gut instincts take over and I moved over beside her on the couch and put my arm around her. It must have been the right thing to do as she stopped cryin' and eventually said that she would be proud to marry me. We went out in the sittin' room where her Pa was waitin' and I asked him if I could marry her just to be polite and make her feel good. He held out his hand and I gave him a handshake. He offered to buy us a home in town but she refused. She said that I was a farmer and that was what she would be, too. It didn't take me long to find out that your mother was a trooper. She held her head high and acted like everything was normal as apple pie. She was about the best wife anybody could have been to me. And I learned to love her a lot; I sure as shootin' did. And I think she learned to love me, too. I didn't even tell my folks about the baby, but now I'm thinkin' that maybe they knew anyway. They wanted to move to Ohio where my sister lived so we had the whole farmhouse to ourselves. We kept up good relations with her folks and I s'pose her Daddy did what he thought was best for her. I guess we was just lucky that we turned out to like each other. You was born right here in this house in my bedroom and in my bed. When you was a week old, I told her that I wanted to take you outdoors. She was a little uneasy at first, but I told her I wanted to show you around so you would know you lived here. I took you to the barn and showed you the cows and the horses, all the time talking to you and telling you about everything. I took you to the root cellar and showed you all the canned goods that your mother and I had put up. I showed you the stream in the root cellar. I showed you the oak tree and told you that we would put a swing up there for you some day. I showed you the windmill and told you how it worked. I showed you the orchard I had planted earlier that year and told you all about the peaches and apples we would enjoy from the trees. Then before we went in the house, I told you that I was your daddy and nothing else mattered. And it hasn't, Donald, nothin' else has mattered." Donald looked at him then and nodded ever so slightly in agreement. Then it suddenly registered with Donald what this would mean to him in regard to what he had been brooding about. He and Emily were absolutely no blood relation.

Vern said, "This really doesn't solve a whole lot as far as you marryin' her. There's still her husband to be considered.

Donald answered, "I know, but I been thinking' on that, too. I'm pretty sure she likes me. I never kissed her, Pop, but I sure have wanted to. And Uncle Dag says I should get her into my bed and she'll never want to leave. He says we all know that sumpthin' must have happened to her husband or he would have at least written to her."

There were a few minutes of silence between the two men and then Donald said, " Maybe I'll tell Uncle Dag that I'll bring her down to his place to visit before the spring work begins." Vern replied, "I'm sure he'd like that a whole lot. Might score a few points for yourself in the bargain."

Chapter 9

DONALD'S IDEA

Donald was not very swift with his actions. That doesn't mean that his mind was slow. It means that he was more deliberate than impulsive. It took him almost a month to present his idea to Emily. One night at supper, Vern said that he would retire early as he felt a bit puny. The kids were getting ready for bed and Donald stated that he would help with kitchen work tonight. Emily was always glad to hear him say that because it gave her some 'alone' time with Donald. She thoroughly enjoyed hearing about his day, his life, or whatever he wanted to talk about. But then, sometimes she would tell him about her life. She had pretty well covered her life with Harlan and her feelings for him. She had conveyed her sorrow at his disappearance and the angst it caused her sometimes not to know.

Donald reached for the dish drying towel and said to her, "I been having an idea 'bout Harlan."

"What kind of an idea?" she asked.

"Where you lived, did they have a United States Postal Office?"

"Well, yes, the Wolf Creek Post Office" she answered, wondering what he was getting at.

"When you left Wolf Creek, did you leave word of a forwarding address?"

"No, the postmaster was sick so the Office wasn't open."

"What if Harlan has written you a letter? You been here for 9 months now. Would they keep the letter or would they throw it away? Would they open it and read it?" He kept the thought of someone else writing about Harlan's death to himself.

This was something that had not occurred to her. She had pinned a piece of paper with her address to the inside of his shirt pocket before he left in the event that something bad might happen. Maybe Donald was right. Maybe there would be a piece of mail in Wolf Creek for her. Donald informed her that he would be going into town tomorrow to check for their own mail and pick up some supplies, and that he had a 3 cent stamp to send a letter with if she would write it tonight.

As soon as the work was done, she gathered up a piece of paper, envelope, and pencil that she had seen in the old secretary desk in the parlor. Sitting at the kitchen table, she wrote to the postmaster telling him where she was and asking if she had received any mail. Donald left her to her task and went to the barn to check things out before he went to bed. He was ever so pleased at her response to his idea. She almost acted as if she was as anxious for things to move on as he was.

The next morning she told him that she wanted to go to town with him. School was closed this week on account of the weather and about half of the children's schooling had indeed been done at the kitchen table so far this year. She would supervise the reading and writing, and just as Vern had said, Donald was good at sums. Vern agreed to stay around the house with the children, so Donald and Emily set off in the old truck right after breakfast. Emily couldn't help but be a little excited about the trip, anyway, but when Donald said that they would visit his mother's parents while they were in town, she was thrilled.

When they parked in front of 'Dunsmore's Dry Goods & Groceries', Donald said, "This is my grandparent's store." In reality, he was a little hesitant as this was the first time he had seen them since he learned about his birth, and he wasn't sure what he should say to them. He needn't have worried because when they entered the door, the old white-haired man behind the counter flashed him a hundred dollar smile. Suddenly, everything was just like it had always been and Donald knew that the issue didn't even need to be discussed between them. He introduced Emily and told them she had been living with him and Pop. Floyd looked her over as though he was thinking of purchasing a prime shipment of coffee.

He said, "I'll send the boy that works for me over to the house to tell Clara that you'll be there for lunch. She'll want to see you, too." Emily could see that there was a great deal of affection between Donald and Floyd. They made their purchases of supplies and visited the Post Office where they posted the letter to Wolf Creek and picked up the Morrison's mail. Donald also bought a newspaper for Vern. It was dated a week ago but Vern would read it thoroughly anyway.

It was almost noon by then and Donald drove over to Oakland Street where the Dunsmores lived in a grand old Victorian house with a white picket fence around the yard and a carriage house out in back. As they stepped up onto the front porch, the door opened and there stood a tall woman with white hair, blue eyes like Donald's, small rimless eyeglasses, and a merry smile on her face. "We were wondering when we were ever going to see you again. Is this Emily? We heard about you," addressing Emily. She reached out and embraced Donald in a big hug, then turned to Emily and took her hand, drawing her in the door in a welcoming gesture.

Floyd came home shortly and the lunch hour passed quickly. Emily and Donald recounted the stories about her arrival at the farm and Uncle Dag's discovery about Emily. Donald told them about Joey and Ruthie and how he and Emily had been teaching them a lot at home.

On the way home, Emily became lost in thought. She said, "Donald, if I'm truly Uncle Dag's daughter, then I'm your cousin."

"Do you believe that you really are his daughter?"

"Yes, and not only because he says so. It just feels right. He is a kind old man. I can't discount the fact about the dresses nor can I disclaim his gray eyes and some of his other mannerisms."

"Then I have something to tell you." And he tried telling it just as Vern had told it to him, leaving out the journey that Vern had made around the farm with a week-old-baby in his arms. That part was too personal. Maybe some day he would tell her.

"So, you see, we are no relation at all. I want to marry you, Emily. I never had a girl before and sometimes I don't know what to do with a woman but I'm tryin' to learn. About the only thing I can think to do sometimes is what I would do with my mother. And I know that you don't want to be treated like my mother."

"Well, Donald, I think you and Vern both loved and respected your mother very much, so being treated like your mother right now is not really a hardship at all. And we still have to wait until we see if we can find out something about Harlan."

"I think about if one of the men that comes along and stops for a meal would be him. What would I do? I know what I would want to do. I would want to start walking back the lane and never stop. I love you that much, Emily. It would kill me to see you with another man."

"I've been thinking about this, too, Donald. If I don't hear anything about Harlan by next summer, I think I have to make a choice. He can't be declared dead for 7 years, but we could make a choice to have a common-law marriage. I think they are just as good as legal. I am not dead and neither are you, but life is passing us by."

"All right, Emmy-girl, let's give it until June 1st. That's about when you came here."

Chapter 10

DAG'S HOUSE

By February everybody was pretty well housebound. The spring work would start about the first of April and from then on there would be no time to visit Dag in his own home. There was still snow on the ground and Donald gave some thought to taking the sleigh. However, it was 40 miles and his passengers might get pretty cold. So, he made sure the old truck was in tip-top shape and planned on starting out after breakfast on Monday morning. He had asked Vern if he wanted to go, but Vern declined, saying that he had some little jobs that needed to be taken care of. The truth was that he didn't want to be a fifth wheel where Donald and Emily were concerned. He didn't think they needed him along to have a good time.

When they were ready to leave, Emily indicated that he should take the bushel basket sitting by the back door. "What's in here?" asked Donald as he lifted the basket. "Why, food, of course, Uncle Dag probably doesn't even know we're coming." She reminded him so much of his mother that he gave a hearty laugh. He said, "Dag knows! I posted him a letter last time I was in town."

"We might want something to eat on the way," she said. Donald laughed again, "A whole bushel basket full? We'll be there in two hours." Emily looked surprised. "How come it took Dag so long to get here?" she asked. Donald laughed some more. "I guess it was because he had Old Runaway Prancer." Then Emily started laughing and since laughter is infectious, Joey, Ruthie, and Vern all started laughing. The adventure was off to a happy start.

Dag lived near Gulchy Gap and the kids could hardly wait to see a town with a name like that. As they drew nearer Donald suddenly turned quite sober. He said there was something he ought to tell them before they got there. Dag's house wasn't anything like theirs was. When his wife and little girl disappeared, it took the spirit right out of him. He had never done much to improve it and so they needed to be prepared so they wouldn't say anything to hurt his feelings.

"Is it bad?" asked Emily.

"Depends on what you mean by bad. It's not bad to him. He's managed to make it livable and he keeps it clean, but it is a log cabin. He has an outhouse out back Our house is quite modern because Pop wanted nice things for my mother, so we have the washroom and running water, but Dag doesn't have that. When you need to use the 'necessary', you have to go to the outhouse." He was speaking to the kids more than to Emily. "He'll probably give you and the kids his bedroom and he and I will bunk in the loft. He doesn't have curtains at the window and just barely has enough dishes for himself, but we will make do and pretend we don't notice. OK, kids?" They agreed and secretly wondered if it was more of an adventure than they had originally thought it to be.

They passed through the little town of Elmore and Donald said, "Only about ten more miles. We should be there in about half an hour." The kids began to peer closely at every house that came in sight as if it might be Uncle Dag's house. At one place a big black dog ran out to the road and barked menacingly at the truck but did not offer to chase it. When they came up over a hill and Donald saw a log cabin all whitewashed neatly, he was confused. Had he missed Dag's place? How could he do that? He had been here before many times. Then he caught sight of an old mule out by the barn. OLD PRANCER! He stopped the truck and looked over the rest of the buildings. They were all whitewashed neatly, too-even the outhouse. He just sat there in the middle of the road until Emily said, "Donald, what is the matter? Are we out of gas?"

He turned slowly into the driveway. Emily was speechless. She had been led to believe that Dag's place was a shambles and she shouldn't expect much. Just then the door opened and Dag stepped out and waved at them to come on in. Emily realized then that Donald had not been putting her on. Dag must have made a super human effort because they were coming to visit. Donald picked up the basket of food from the back of the truck and they all started toward the house. Dag looked like the cat that ate the canary as he stood back and let them enter. There were yellow print curtains at every window and a whole new set of dishes on the shelf along with cutlery. The cook stove had a new coat of blacking on it and there was a tablecloth on the table. Not only that, but there were six chairs around the table. True, they were homemade but nevertheless a place for everyone to sit. Emily looked out the window toward the barn and swore she could see a scrap of yellow print at the window. Dag had even put a curtain up for Old Prancer. She felt a laugh rising up inside of her and when she looked at Donald, the fat was in the fire. He, too, had seen the curtain in the barn window; they started laughing and it wasn't long before everybody, including Dag was laughing helplessly.

Chapter 11

THE VISIT

Donald and the children had gone to the barn to see Old Prancer's new curtains and Emily was unpacking the basket of food she had brought along. There was fried chicken and two cans of peaches and a can of green beans, plus two apple pies. Dag let loose with his funny little cackle and said, "Now, Emmy-girl, ya didn't figger I would have anything' for ya to eat, did ya?"

Emily's face reddened slightly and she said, "Well, I didn't know, Uncle Dag, but I sure did want to see where I lived when I was a little girl. Are you doubtful at all about me being your daughter?" Dag picked up her right hand and turned it over. There in the middle of her palm was a scar about a quarter of an inch long. She had always wondered what it was from but her parents didn't know either. He said, "Just a month or so before ya left, ya was playin' around a fence post out by the barn and ya put yer hand down on a piece of broken glass. It cut one of them auteries inside ya that carries blood from yer heart. The blood just spurted out like somebody was pumpin' it and I thought ya was goin' to bleed to death. But yer mother knew what to do. She wrapped her arms around ya and put her thumb on the cut and just pressed it right there for about half an hour. When she finally let go of it, the blood had clotted and she put a bandage on it. Then we watched it to see that it didn't start bleedin' again."

"She must have loved me," Emily said, "What do you think happened to her? Why did she leave me on a stranger's doorstep? Why did she run away from you?" Dag looked thoughtful for a minute and then he said, "At first I thought she was just evil to take my little girl away from me. I never figgered that she had any spleen against me. I think that drummer fellow just charmed her and spirited her away. She was a good, hard working' woman and it surprised me no end when she did what she did. She was Vern's sister. What does he have to say about it?"

She said, "I asked him once and he said it was painful to talk about it but he decided that I had a right to know. He told me that he had two sisters, Henrietta and Florence. The girls were his Pa's pride and joy, he was more his Ma's boy, but his Pa treated him all right. When Henrietta ran away with little Maybelle it near killed his Ma and Pa both. They kept watching in the mail for news from her until they moved to Ohio. And Vern watched even after that. Vern don't believe that she would have ever left me on a stranger's doorstep. He thinks she must have died for some reason and the drummer left me there. Frank and Mary Anderson would have been happy to know what kind of people I came from. They were good people and saw to it that I had a good education. Donald says that maybe some day when times are better, we can hire a detective to find out what happened to her."

"What's happenin' with you and Donald?" he asked. "I kinda see that there is sumpthin' a little different between you." "Yes," she said, "I have written a letter to the post office at Wolf Creek to see if Harlan or anybody else has written to me. If I haven't heard from him by June 1st, we will enter into a common-law marriage agreement. Time is passing us by, and I can't have Harlan declared dead until 7 years after I have heard from him. I feel in my heart that he is dead. It wouldn't have been like him to abandon us. Donald has been one of the best men I have ever known." There was such a long silence that she thought the conversation was over. Then Dag put his hand on her shoulder and said, "Donald is a good man. He would never leave your younguns on a stranger's doorstep." She thought it probably was as close to a hug as she was apt to get. She nodded her head slightly and thought how strange it was that she had picked up one of Donald's mannerisms.

That night at bedtime, Dag was assigning places to sleep. He gave Emily and Ruthie his bedroom to sleep in and to her surprise it had a comfortable bed and what looked to be a new quilt. When she asked him about it, he said that his Mama had made it for him and Henrietta and when she and Donald entered into their agreement, it would be theirs. She told him that she would be very pleased to have it. Then he looked at Joey and said, "Son, why don't ya bring yer blanket up to the loft with us men. Yer too big to sleep with yer mother and sister." Joey happily picked up his blanket from the bedroom floor and went up the ladder to the loft. Donald was already up there and had claimed one of the two mattresses on the floor. When Joey started to spread his blanket on the floor, Donald said, " Why don't you crawl in here with me? This mattress is big enough for both of us."

After breakfast the next morning, which consisted of ham, eggs and homemade biscuits, Dag took them all on a tour of his property. First he showed them the barn and they all admired Old Prancer's yellow curtains. There was a cow in the box stall and hay up in the loft. Then there was the smokehouse, which had a good supply of hams in it; after that, the root cellar with shelves full of garden booty that Dag said he had canned himself. He showed them the garden although, all they could see right now was that it was a good size. No, even if he was a bit strange, Dag certainly wasn't lazy. She saw a frayed rope hanging from a box elder tree and knew that it had been a swing for her.

Then he harnessed Old Prancer and hitched her to the sleigh and took them on a tour around the square mile. He let Joey sit in the front seat with the men and hold the reins. He secretly hoped that some day the children would call him 'Grandpa'.

Donald had told Vern before they left that they would stay one night but not to worry if they stayed a second night. He had an idea that Emily would want to poke her nose into everything about Dag's place and it might take more than one day. He was right. Emily knew that she would come to love this old man a whole lot. Vern and Donald seemed to think a lot of him, too.

The second day, after another big farmer's breakfast, the guests were getting ready to leave, when Dag said he had an errand to do outside. Donald went out with him and Emily watched them out of the kitchen window as they caught one of the three red banty roosters that were scratching around the yard. He had several banty hens, which were not too great for eating as they were small chickens but were great for eggs. He put a rooster and a hen in a burlap bag and Donald put it in the truck behind the seat so they wouldn't freeze to death on the way home. He told Ruthie that she wouldn't want to play with the rooster as that kind of chicken was feisty and it might take offense and attack her.

They started off for home and the kids were looking out the window taking in all of the scenery, when Donald turned to Emily and pursed his lips into a kiss. Her face reddened again but he had, in fact, kissed her twice already and she welcomed the thought of having it happen again.

Chapter 12

DONALD'S DILEMMA

It had been almost a year since God and the old car had planted the Jones family on the Morrison's front porch. Emily had quickly put the old concept of 'Make yourself indispensable' to work and she and the kids did indeed make themselves indispensable. She and Ruthie had launched right into harvesting and canning the garden produce. Joey, delighted to be working with the men, made himself useful in the fields and in the barn. Vern, still lonesome from the loss of his Flora the year before, enjoyed the evenings exchanging small talk with the other members of the family. He was great with the children, and encouraged Ruthie's chatter whenever the occasion arose. Both he and Donald relished the meals that Emily put before them. He had become more convinced that Dag was right about Emily. Dag had claimed to know something instantly when he first saw Emily, but Vern was not easily convinced. It just didn't seem that anything in life could be so simple that his sister's long-lost daughter could be thrown away 500 miles from home and land on his front porch 27 years later. He just did not believe that things happened like that. Still- the things that Dag had based his belief on seemed to be rightful. The scar on the palm of her hand was something he remembered vividly. He and his family had been there at Dag's house the day it happened. And how could he explain the coincidence of the dresses and the doll dress all made of the same flowery material. She certainly had Dag's gray eyes and even his dimple at the right corner of her mouth.

Donald was another matter. He had started to fall in love with her the first few days she was there. Then came the disappointment with Dag's discovery which would have made them cousins, followed by the disclosure from Vern about Donald's birth, which made the world flop right side up again. The problem was that Donald had been to school and had a good education, but there was no school to learn about women, and he often felt like a square peg in a round hole where Emily was concerned. Sometimes when they were having a private conversation, she would give him a smile that made him feel all warm and fuzzy. He finally decided that he needed to talk to another man and get some masculine advice. But, who? He thought Vern might know the best thing to do, but it would be very hard to admit to his father that he was so lacking in expertise. He loved his grandfather dearly, but doubted if he even remembered what it was like to be young and uncertain. If only his mother was here, she would be able to shed some light on his problem. Then a thought hit him like a lightning bolt. What about Grandmother Clara? She usually came up with some good ideas.

The next day he went to town to get the mail and stopped around to visit her. She could see right away that he had something on his mind. It wasn't lunchtime yet but she brewed a pot of coffee and they sat down at the kitchen table. After a little mundane talk while Donald was trying to think how to broach the subject, Clara said, "Well, Donald, let's hear what you've got to say, and don't tell me it's nothing. I know you better than that." It startled him once again that his grandmother could get to the bottom of a problem so quickly and he found himself talking freely to her about Emily and his feelings for her.

She said, "I've been keeping my eye on you two, and I see you cutting your eyes back and forth at each other. It's about time you realized that you can't ignore this any more than you could ignore lack of breath."

"But, Grandmother," he replied, "There is an 'elephant in the kitchen'* and his name is Harlan. How can we just ignore him? How can we wait 7 years to have him declared dead when Em and I are both in our 30's? I can accept Joey and Ruthie but I want a child or children of my own."

"Have you and Emily discussed this? Has she given you any indication as to how she feels about this?"

"I guess I've had indications, but don't ask me what they are. I don't know. I think she does just from the way she does special little things for me and the way she looks at me sometimes and makes me feel."

Clara was lost in thought for a few moments and then asked, "Have you ever given her little presents? I mean like a pretty stone that you found in the field or an especially pretty leaf that you found on the ground in the fall? Did you ever pick a bouquet of wildflowers and bring to her?" She arose from her chair and went into the parlor. When she came back, she had her old family Bible in her hand. She opened it and there was a small bunch of flowers pressed between two pieces of tissue paper. "Your grandfather brought me these one day when we were expecting our Flora. I was so touched by his little sentimental gesture, that I preserved them like this." She seemed to be thinking about what she wanted to say next. "Did you ever share a secret place that you especially like with her? Did you ever share secrets about yourself with her?" Then, with a look of enlightenment on her face, she said, "Did you ever see a book on the shelf in your parlor called 'A Tale of Two Cities'? I'd wager that tucked into the pages of that book you will find another bouquet like this that your father gave to your Mom the day you were born. She showed them to me once."

Donald was greatly impressed. He had taken Emily and the kids up to the orchard last fall when the Hunter's Moon had been full and told them all that he knew about the stars in the sky. They had all seemed to enjoy it and the kids had asked him when he was going to do it again. The Grandfather clock in the hall chimed the noon hour and Clara went to the kitchen to start lunch. Donald followed her, as he knew he could never get away without spending a little time with Floyd.

She continued the conversation they had started. "We really haven't touched much on the most important subject which, of course, is the elephant in the kitchen." She conversed about all the possibilities concerning Harlan and Donald tucked all that she said away in a corner of his brain for later thought. He realized that he was in the midst of a life-altering situation and he didn't want to do anything rash.

After lunch, he left the Dunmore home and finished his errands in town. When he turned in the drive at home, Emily came out on the porch and waved at him. He knew in that moment that whatever he did with her, it would be the right thing.

Chapter 13

DONALD'S QUEST

After supper that night Donald retired to the parlor to search out 'A Tale of Two Cities', and sure enough, there it was right on the top shelf of the bookcase. Carefully, he took it down and it opened right up to a small bouquet of dried flowers. There was a note between the pages in Flora's handwriting that said, "June 15, 1901, Vern brought me these wildflowers from the woods today. He said they were for giving him a son. I love him more every day." Donald stood for a short time just staring at the crumbling flowers, and then went to the kitchen where Emily and Vern were finishing up the supper dishes. He laid the book on the table and asked Vern if he knew about the flowers. He said, "Yes, and I wish they weren't disintegrating like they are. Your mother was so pleased the day I brought them to her." Emily came over to see what they were talking about and her face lit up with excitement.

"When I was in town the other day, there was a new product in the grocery store. It was called waxed paper, and it is to wrap sandwiches in to keep them fresh, but while I was looking at it, another woman said that she pressed flowers between two pieces with a flatiron. The wax stuck the two pieces of paper together. I could try it if you would get some of the paper." A worried look crossed her face, and she continued, "But if it didn't work, then you would lose them."

Vern pondered this for a bit and said, " I guess there's nothing to lose. They're crumbling anyway. We'll get some of this paper next time we're in town and you can see what you can do with them."

Donald continued to rack his brain for new ways to court Emily. Oh, he tried all the things that had been done by the men in his family but not with a lot of success. He continued to help her clean up after supper mainly so he would have some alone time with her. The fact that Ruthie was busy with her lessons was to his advantage. He brought her an occasional wildflower or an arrowhead that he found back in the fields. He took her and the kids back to the orchard on nights of the full moon and told them all the lore he knew about the moon and stars. And they seemed to enjoy these forays into the heavens but so far nothing had even remotely moved 'the elephant in the kitchen'.

A couple of nights later, Donald was helping in the kitchen with clean up when a drinking glass slipped out of Emily's hands and shattered on the floor. He grabbed the broom and Emily went for the mop and mop pail in the bathroom and pantry. As he was sweeping, he noticed smears of blood on the floor. She came back into the kitchen limping and he took her tools and helped her to a chair while he examined her feet. Imagine his surprise when he discovered holes worn clear through the bottom of her shoes. Vern had seen to it that the kid's feet were shod with decent shoes, but nobody had noticed Emily's feet. Well, maybe Pop had noticed but was waiting for Donald to do something about it. As he tended to the cuts on one foot and pulled a shard of glass out of the flesh on the other, his mind was whirling. When he had some fairly awkward bandages in place, he picked her up and carried her upstairs to her bedroom. "Now, you get ready and get in bed. I'll look in on you before I go to bed."

Back downstairs, Vern was finishing the dishes and putting them away, so Donald mopped the kitchen floor to remove all the glass. Then he picked up her shoes and looked at them again. By Cracky! If money wasn't so tight, he would go right to town tonight and have Grandfather open the Dry Goods Store and buy her a pair of shoes. There were probably shoes from his mother in the attic but Emily had a substantially larger foot than Flora, so that would never do. Then he knew what he would do. There was a shoe repair box out in the tack room in the barn that they had used to keep the family shoes in good repair for as long as Donald could remember. He left for the barn with the shoes and an hour later, came back to the house with a pair of shoes with new half-soles made out of harness leather on them. He took them up to Emily's room and set them beside the bed. She and Ruthie were sleeping peacefully and he wondered if he dared to kiss her on the forehead. He decided not to take a chance.

The next morning when he came into the kitchen for breakfast, Emily was standing at the stove with her back to him. He sat down at the table and was drinking his first cup of coffee when he realized that Emily was crying. He went to her and set the breakfast pans in the warming oven, then put his arms around her. As she turned to him, she burst into tears and sobbed her heart out. Donald must have had a vision, because he did exactly the right thing. He just let her cry while he held her. When the sobs began to wind down, he said, "Tell me about it, sweetheart and I'll see if I can fix it." She stopped crying and replied, "It has been so long since anyone did something so thoughtful just for me, I just don't know how to handle it. I think I love you, Donald." I think it's time we came to some kind of resolution about us. My adopted mother used to say that nine-tenths of the eggs that are laid are never hatched. We can't live out our lives on the premise that *maybe* Harlan will come back. If he does, we'll have to face it then. Even if he couldn't get work, he would have let me know if he was alive."

Chapter 14

THE COMMITMENT

The spring work had been under way for about a month now. The plowing and planting were almost finished in the grain fields. There was still the corn to be planted and then they would tackle the garden. Donald, and sometimes Vern, would sit in the kitchen while she and Ruthie did the clean-up chores. Joey had pretty much taken over the barn chores, so Emily had decreed that the men were off the hook for housework. All three of them were doing their share of work in the fields and in the barn.

One night they were almost finished with only Donald and Emily in the kitchen and Donald said, "I wish you were coming to bed with me, Emily. Do you remember the promise you made?"

"Of course I do. Did you think I would forget? Or did you think I would break my word?"

"I guess I'm just afraid it won't happen."

She went over to him and kissed him tenderly on the lips. Their kissing had accelerated and happened quite frequently now. Donald had made up his mind that he wasn't such a washout at things romantic after all.

"There is only one thing that would stop me, and you know what that is."

"When do you think we might hear from the postmaster at Wolf Creek?"

"I have no idea, but it does seem like if there was anything to tell me, they would have sent it by now."

"I guess we're just going to have to live our whole life with Harlan hanging over us."

"What other choice do we have, Donald?"

"None, as far as I can see. I don't want to live out my life as an old bachelor, and I don't want any other woman."

"Well, I guess we'll just have to live on the edge, then. But I'm not certain how to proceed. Are we supposed to make an announcement? Should we draw up a contract? Should we have some kind of a ceremony? Or do we just say that on June 1st we are going to climb into bed together and that's it?"

Donald laughed and said, "Maybe all of the above."

"What does Vern say about it?"

"Maybe we'd better ask him about it."

The next evening, Donald asked Vern to stay around after the kids had gone to bed. When Vern inquired as to what the issue was, Emily said, "You do know what we are planning on the first of June, don't you?" Then Donald told him what their concerns were, saying that he knew the whole thing was not traditional, but they felt it was the only thing left to them. Vern sat silently for a few moments looking at his hands, then said, "We've always been God-fearing people. I don't know what your mother would say. Somehow I think she would give you her blessing. These are desperate times, and sometimes desperate times call for desperate measures. I don't know the answers to your questions, but I do know somebody that might. Have you talked to your Grandfather Dunsmore about this? They're going to have to know. Donald acknowledged that they hadn't, but thought maybe Vern was right. He and Emily would visit them and ask their advice.

Joey and Ruthie were going to school almost every day now that the weather was nicer. Joey had mastered the art of riding Topsy and since she was too old to do farm work she was free for the ride. Using the saddle Donald had given him for Christmas with Ruthie behind hanging onto him it worked out fine. The teacher who was a good sized man promised to help them onto the horse to send them home each day.

Donald said that he needed some seed corn so they would make the trip to town tomorrow. The first place they stopped was at Dunsmore's Dry Goods where Floyd greeted them joyfully. He was just as happy to see Vern as he was the other two. He always prided himself on making a good choice for his daughter when he picked Vern Morrison. He inquired as to what their plans were. He knew that this was a busy time of the year and didn't know whether they would be staying for lunch or not. Clara would be disappointed if they didn't but she would understand. Donald told him that they had a matter to discuss with him, and would like to have a couple of hours of his time. He sent his assistant over to tell Clara to have lunch ready. He thought that Vern and Donald were doing pretty good but maybe they wanted to borrow some money.

Emily stayed in the store and ordered the food staples she needed while the other two went to the Feed and Seed Store When they arrived at the house on Oakland Street, they were met at the door by two rather long faces. Not wanting to keep them in suspense about his dilemma, Donald launched into their problem as soon as they sat down to lunch. Floyd and Clara heard him out and Floyd said that there wasn't any protocol to a common-law marriage as far as he knew. He understood why they were taking this way of joining their lives, but wished it could be different. They both liked Emily and had been hoping that Donald would find a good woman and settle down.

Clara had been quietly thinking about what they had told and suddenly, her whole being lit up. She said, "Why, Floyd, what is the matter with you? Of course there is a protocol, at least there will be at this wedding. The first of June, you say?" True to form, Donald nodded his head slightly. Clara continued, "We'll have a ceremony right here in our parlor. It will not be a marriage ceremony. It will be a commitment ceremony. I will write the words myself and Floyd can perform the vows." Floyd was looking like a gigged frog about now. He began to protest and Clara said, "And you can draw up a contract for them to sign, Floyd. I'm sure you can figure out what to say in it." At her last words, Floyd began to catch her enthusiasm. He addressed Vern and said, "Do you still have Flora's wedding dress?" Clara jumped in again, " I have it right up here in our attic. She wanted me to take care of it after her wedding, so we have it here. I'll get it down and see if we can make it do." "No, no," Emily protested, "I have just made myself a new dress from some cloth that Vern and Donald gave me for Christmas. I really wouldn't feel right about wearing a white wedding dress." Clara turned to Emily and said, "You be sure and invite your father to come." For just a minute Emily didn't know what she was talking about and then it hit her. She meant Dag- yes, her father.

They got into the truck to go home with Emily sitting in the middle. Donald turned toward her and pursed his lips into a kiss. As he looked up, his eye caught Vern looking straight ahead and grinning for all he was worth.

That night after supper, Emily excused herself early and went upstairs with Joey and Ruthie. The three of them were sitting in her bedroom with their nightclothes on, and Emily got right to the business at hand.

"We have talked about the possibility of your father never coming back. I am quite sure that if he were alive we would have heard from him or he would be back with us. Donald wants me to marry him."

Joey spoke up, "How can you do that, Mom? Dad may still come back."

"I couldn't marry him legally, but there are a lot of people in the same position that we are. There is a thing called common-law marriage. It is not legal but it is a commitment that two people make to each other. We were going to your Aunt Jane's in Virginia to live with them because we were on our way to starving to death. They were having a hard time, too and didn't really want us. They were going to take us in out of kindness, but we would have been charity. Here we can earn our own way, by working with Donald and Vern."

Joey was silent for a moment and then he said, "You're in love with Donald, aren't you, Mom?" When she nodded her head, he continued, "I like Donald and Vern both. It is real nice working with them doing man's work. They treat Ruthie and me so nice and we haven't been hungry once since we've been here."

Ruthie could be quiet no longer. "Will you be sleeping with Donald? Can I have the bedroom all to myself? Will we have to call him Daddy? Oh, Mama, could we have a baby?"

All three were quiet with their own thoughts when Joey said, "I think Dad would want us to go on with our lives and be happy."

Chapter 15

THE PALLADIUM THEATER

It was the second week in May and Vern had worked up the soil in the garden and worked some fertilizer from the manure pile into it and it was ready to plant. Early in February the three of them had pored over the seed catalogs and ordered what they needed. Emily had said that some day when times were better and they could afford it, she would like to plant a few zinnias. They were so colorful. When the box of seeds had arrived, there tucked down in the corner was a packet of zinnia seeds. She looked at Donald and he just shrugged, but she knew that he was the one who had ordered them. Now, on the 12th of May in a full moon, they had the garden all planted.

The 1st of June was drawing closer and Clara had told Emily that she and Floyd were giving them a night at the Grand Hotel in Perryville on their commitment night. Emily hadn't told Donald yet as she thought they might want to surprise him. Her dress was all ready and she had even found a piece of cloth to make Ruthie a new dress. The men had both bought new suits for Flora's funeral and she took them from the closet and pressed them. Donald had taken Joey to town on Monday and bought him some new pants and shoes. They had received a letter from Dag last week saying that he would try to arrive on May 30th or 31st, according to what Old Prancer wanted to do. Emily wondered what his attire for this event would look like. Vern assured her that it would be clean. Ruthie who had indeed learned to patch clothes said that if he wore the overalls with the strange looking patch on them, she would spirit them away from him and put a nice patch on the knee.

On the 30th of the month, excitement was running amok. Emily was afraid that Dag wouldn't get there in time, but she needn't have worried. Just as they were sitting down to eat that night she looked out at the road and recognized Old Prancer. She was pulling an old wagon with one smaller wheel on the front. The seat that Dag was sitting on looked dangerously slanty to Emily, but she had come to accept almost anything that he might do with composure. As she watched, she realized there was some kind of a big object in the wagon covered with a blanket. She called, "Donald! Vern! Come quick. Dag is here and I think he might need some help." They went out to see what was going on and Emily set another place at the table. When she went out to greet Dag, he had a big sheepish grin on his face. He was telling the men that he and Old Prancer had started out at 6 o'clock this morning and they had made pretty good time considering that he had let the old mule rest and eat 4 times on the trip. The men had been lifting the blanket and looking at what was underneath it. She could see that he wanted her to look, too. When she lifted the blanket, her eyes nearly popped out of her head. It was a pump organ- quite a grand one, in fact. Vern and Donald must have told him what she said that first day about playing the organ. Vern said, "Why don't ya just drive this wagon right in the barn and we'll unload it in the morning'?" That seemed satisfactory to everyone and they went in to supper.

"How did you come by the organ, Uncle Dag? Emily asked, "I didn't see one in your house when we were there.

"Well, they're tearin' the old Palladium Theater down in Gulchy Gap and they was goin' to throw it in the dump. So I went in and tried it out and couldn't see nothing' much wrong with it, so I offered 'em $3 for it and they was tickled pink. I remembered that Donald told me about you offering to play the organ to pay for somethin' to eat when you first came here, so here it is. Maybe you can play somethin' for us when we get it in here. You need to be decidin' where you want us to put it"

He looked from one to another and back again. They were all standing there like God had struck them dumb. Finally, Emily found her tongue and said, "You said you went in and tried it."

"Well, sure, now, girl, you don't think I would give them $3 for it unless I knew it worked, do ya?" Images of Uncle Dag playing the organ were hovering over the supper table like a swarm of mosquitoes over a swamp. Dag continued, "I coulda made that old organ jump in my younger days. Don't do too bad now, if I do say so myself. Brought along my organ tuning tools and I'll have it soundin' just like downtown afore I leave here. May need to replace some felts, but I can do that, too. Brought some linseed oil to polish it up, too." Donald said, "I can't wait, Uncle Dag, if we go out to the barn can you play it right now on the wagon?" "Sure can, boy!" so before the table was even cleaned up they all trooped out to the barn where Uncle Dag played 'When the Saints Come Marching In'. He didn't just play it; he played it 'spiritedly'.

Chapter 16

THE COMMITMENT CEREMONY - 1932

The next day passed swiftly with everybody busy getting ready for the festivities. The organ was still on the wagon in the barn but Emily had told the men where she wanted it placed in the parlor. Uncle Dag had asked Emily if he could use her iron and ironing board. He wanted to press his suit. Emily said, "Uncle Dag, you are so full of surprises. I didn't even know you had a suit, and furthermore I didn't know you could iron it."

"What do you think, girl, that I just fell off the turnip truck?"

"I think that I am just beginning to find out who you are. And I will press it for you. I have never pressed my father's suit before and I will consider it a privilege."

The next morning after breakfast everyone began to spruce themselves up, as they needed to be at the Dunsmore's house by 1 o'clock. At first, Joey had objected to his mother joining with Donald because he still held out hope that his father would come back into their lives. Donald had taken him out to the barn and tried to give him a different view of the proceedings. Joey had cheered up a little bit and said that he liked Donald and Vern enough. It was just so doubtful about his dad. Donald said he understood and it was still doubtful for his mother.

Emily's surprises were not all revealed yet. Dag and Vern got into the truck and made room for Joey and Ruthie. Emily said to Donald, "I thought they were going to sit in the back. Do we have to get in the back of the truck?" Donald smiled slightly and grabbed her hand and kept right on going to the barn. He opened the barn door and there sat her old car with a spit and polish on it she had never seen before. Donald said, "How did you think we were going to the hotel tonight without the rest of them if we only had the truck?"

"How did you know about the hotel?"

"I didn't just fall off the turnip truck yesterday, either."

Emily laughed and then she thought of something. "How long has this car been fixed?"

"Oh, quite a while."

"Why didn't you tell me about it?"

"I told you I didn't fall off the turnip—"

She interrupted him: "You knew I was anxious about it."

"Emily, you haven't been very anxious about anything. Besides, I didn't want you to get any ideas about leaving here." She considered what he had said and conceded that he was right. Well, that was all over. As of today, she was not going to think about going anywhere without Donald.

Floyd and Clara did indeed have a celebration planned. Clara had written a special set of rites following the traditional wedding ceremony quite closely. Floyd stood in front of the fireplace in the parlor and administered them. Donald looked so handsome and happy. Emily hardly dared to look at Dag. She had trimmed his beard and hair for him and he actually looked handsome, too. Floyd had drawn up a Contract Of Commitment that he had them sign when the ceremony was over and Donald had actually come up with a silver wedding band that was his mother's. Donald would have been content to go to the hotel immediately after Clara had handed him a card telling him about it, but Emily gave him a look that said, "Behave yourself!"

Three of the ladies from Clara's church had helped her prepare a marvelous dinner and as they sat down to the table, Emily was in for another surprise. Uncle Dag wanted to say the blessing. He said, "Thank ya, Lord, for this bounteous meal, but thank ya most of all for the gatherin' of this family. Amen!"

The food was passed around and everybody filled their plate. Then Emily said, "I have something that has been on my mind for a while. Joey and Ruthie and my relationship to all of you has changed today." She looked at the children and said, "Since Donald is now my husband, I think it would be nice if you didn't call him Donald any more. What would you like to call him?" Ruthie piped up and said, "I want to call Vern 'Pop' because that's what D- he calls him." and she pointed at Donald. Joey nodded his head. Dag spoke up then and said, "I want to be called 'Grandpa'" and he looked at the kids. Looking at Emily, he said, "And, Emmy-girl, I think it's time you called me who I am. I'm your Pa" Emily then said, "I'll call Vern 'Pop', too"

Donald, feeling a little bit left out, said, "That still leaves me the odd man out. Nobody wants to call me anything." Ruthie started giggling and said, "I think we should all call him Mr. Morrison." Everybody laughed heartily, but Joey spoke to Donald then, "Ruthie and I will call you Donald, if that's all right with you." He looked down at the floor, and said, "As far as we know, we still have a Pa." Donald winked at him and said that would be all right. If he was disappointed, no one knew it. As an afterthought, Emily said, "I think we should call Mr. and Mrs. Dunsmore Grandfather and Grandmother." Everyone was happy with their new names.

Chapter 17

DAG'S ADVENTURE

The merry talk continued until it came around to the subject of the new organ. Dag was implored to repeat the story of how he happened to buy the organ. After telling it one more time, he settled back like he had more to say. Emily sensed that they were about to be royally entertained. This is the story he told:

"When I was just a tad, we was pretty poor. My Ma and Pa wanted a big family and they set about to have it. She said they was always a babe in her arms or one on the way. I had five brothers and two sisters all older than me. There was Taggert, Claggett, Bell, twins Barrett and Garrett, then 2 girls, Agnes and Maggie. Ma's name was Agatha and she was a looker, she was! Pa named Tag, Clag, Dag, Agnes, and Maggie with a ag in each name cause he was so crazy about Ma. Bell was Ma's maiden name so she named Bell and she named the twins because her ma's maiden name was Barrett and Garrett rhymed with it. I had problems with my breathin' so I had to stay in the house a lot. Don't think for a minute that I was allowed to waste my time. My sisters taught me how to cook, clean, and sew. Yeah, they even taught me to iron clothes. Little Missy is thinkin' that they didn't teach me to do a knee patch very pretty and she's right. Somehow I had it in mind that it wouldn't be in my best interests to do it up real pretty. Pa was a hard worker and so was Ma and they didn't have too much money or time to play. Ma taught me to play the old pump organ in the parlor and I musta' had some sort of music flair 'cause I picked it right up. Then I began to tinker with it to make it play better and afore they knew what's happening, I 'quired a set of organ tunin' tools. My breathin' got better as I got older and I started workin' outside with Pa and my brothers."

"Well, I musta' been in my teens and I was startin' to think about girls. We lived in Cobb County, Georgia near Mayretta. They was lots of talk about buildin' a new thee-ay-ter on the square in town. They started buildin' it and ever time one of us went to town, that would be all we talked about at supper that night. It was gonna' be called 'The Strand' and it was gonna' be grander than anythin' else in town. It was said that when the Chautauqua singers came to town they would use the thee-ay-ter and also traveling preachers would hold revivals there. But the big thing was that there would be movin' picture shows. Now, my Pa was just spellbound by the thought of pitchers up on the wall movin' around. He swore to my Ma that when that thee-ay-ter was all done, he would take us to the Grand Openin'.

It took about a year to build it and the Grand Openin' was set for June 1st of 1898. Two of my brothers, Tag and Clag lived close and they had families so Pa made up a Grand Party of about 15 people to go to the Grand Openin'. Now, we just had two old mules to work the farm with, so Pa put some boards up along the sides of the wagon and hitched Cain and Abel up to pull it. Since there wasn't no seats Pa and my brothers had put kitchen chairs and a couple of easy chairs, whatever kind of chair that was movable, on the wagon bed. For some reason, Pa hadn't thought to put a barricade across the back, probably thinking' that he'd have a harder time gettin' them mules to even move forward let alone run.

We lived about 6 miles out of town so it took a while to get there and we had just entered the square and Pa was looking for some place to tether the team when the Marchin' Band started playin'. They was playin' some lively marchin' tune and they just started out with a bang. Scared old Cain half to death. Now, there ain't nothin' to a runaway mule but two runaway mules is somethin' to be reckoned with. Me and the twins was sittin' across the back and we fell out into the dirt right away. Ma's chair started to slide to the back and Pa put his foot out to stop it and made it tip over. Pa had all he could do to get the team under control. Ma grabbed one of the little kids with one hand and tried to hang on to the side rack with the other, but she lost her shoe. I picked it up as I ran past so it wasn't a total loss. One of the little boys had grabbed a hold of her ankles and was screamin' for dear life. Tag's wife was sittin' in an easy chair aholdin' the babe. She managed to grab a side rail and hang on to the babe at the same time. The two girls was hangin' on to each other but they was almost off the end. I got up out of the dirt and ran after the wagon. I caught up just in time to keep the little girls from flyin' out of the end and Pa got the mules stopped at the same time. Everbody was shook up but nobody was hurt bad. I held the mules while Pa restored order in the wagon. He had everthin' under control and told me to get in the wagon and we would find a place for the mules. I told him I'd just as leave walk.

He just got the mules goin' again when the train come through right next to us and blew the whistle. It set them mules off again, only this time I was on foot. They was twice as much screamin' and brayin' as they was before. Ma's chair tipped over again and this time Ma almost went out the back. She was screamin' "Brown! Brown!" (that's what she called Pa) "You stop them mules right now!" She grabbed onto Clag's ankle and he grabbed onto Tag who grabbed onto the front railin'. Both my sister-in-laws hung onto their kids and nobody fell out. I was runnin' to catch the runaway mules. We got clear down to the edge of town-three blocks, afore I managed to jump onto Cain's back and calm them danged mules down. Pa said, "Everbody get in, we's a going' home." I guess he had enough of the city life, as I never did get to go to the Strand until I went there to tune the organ. Turned out the movin' pitchers was just a stage built high up on the wall with a coupla' girls in it that moved around a little bit; not at all like the movin' pitchers we has today. But people was always askin' me after that if I wasn't one of them Browns that had the runaway mules. "

Everybody had been sitting quiet as a mouse while Dag was telling his story. Now Ruthie giggled and the fat was in the fire. They all laughed until Floyd choked and everyone sobered up.

It was getting along toward chore time so the guests started departing. Donald and Emily left for the night at the hotel. He said, "Emmy, I don't know much about what we're gonna be doing and I don't want to hurt you." "She said, "Just do what you want to, Donald, if you hurt me I'll tell you." And thus their life together as a family started.

Chapter 18

THE PARTNERS

The next morning at breakfast in the hotel dining room, Emily asked Donald what had happened between him and Joey to make Joey accept their situation. "I remembered how I felt when Pop told me about him and my mother. I figured Joey was old enough to begin to put 2 and 2 together about yours and my relationship so I told him the truth just like Pop told it to me. I wanted him to know that people could be happy with put-together families. Then I told him that he knew all about the stream and the orchard and the root cellar so I didn't have to show them to him like Pop did with me when I was a week old. But, maybe there was something he didn't know and that was that we were going to be a family and he was going to be my son, and nothing else mattered at all. Must be I said the right thing because I could see him studyin' Pop and then me. I thought he was convinced, then he surprised the bejabbers out of me when he said he and Ruthie wanted to call me Donald because they already had a Dad. Emily said, "Well, thank you, Donald, for making the effort. I'm probably like most mothers and the happiness of my kids is a main concern of mine. I think if it was just you and me, there wouldn't even be a concern." She smiled at him and his face flushed a little.

"Must be I was all right last night."

She laughed, "Oh, Donald, you were a bit more than all right."

When they arrived at the farm, the kids ran out to greet them, but Vern and Dag made themselves conspicuously absent. Donald asked, "Do you want me to help you put our bedroom in order?" She told him that there wasn't much to do and she thought she could manage it. He changed his clothes and went back to the field to find the men.

Emily busied herself in the bedroom and made a mental list of what she would like to do to make it hers. She put her clothes in the wardrobe and her personal things on the dresser, and then started looking at the room with a more critical eye. It needed a good cleaning and the curtains were sort of droopy. Probably this was Donald's boyhood room and nobody had thought to do much to it. She would definitely like to put up new wallpaper and curtains but that would have to wait until times were a little better. The dresser, bed and chest along with the night table by the bed could be improved with a scrubbing and some polish she had seen in the storeroom downstairs. She started by stripping the bed and washing the sheets. Then she scrubbed and polished the floor and the furniture, and moved the furniture into different positions. She had seen some cloth in Flora's box in the attic that would make some nice fresh curtains for the window. She could enlist Ruthie's help with sewing.

When the men came in for supper, she had a nice stew going on the stove and they made a big fuss over the smell of the kitchen. She and Ruthie had pledged each other to secrecy about the bedroom, so after the meal she said to Donald, "I forgot to take my valise upstairs from staying at the hotel. Would you take it up for me?" He picked it up and Ruthie stifled a giggle. About 5 minutes later, they heard him coming down the stairs. He stood in the kitchen door and stared at Emily, trying to keep a straight face. When Emily couldn't keep quiet any longer, She said, "What's the matter, Donald?" He replied, "Doggies, I thought I was in the wrong room." The girls started laughing and Donald had to take the men upstairs to see what Emily had done. Vern said, "This is real nice, Emily, it needs to be papered, and we'll keep that in mind, when we have a little more money. We can do it ourselves. But I guess there are things we can do to improve the whole house when that happens."

Chapter 19

HARLAN SURFACES - 1934

Everyone settled into the harvesting, both in the fields and the garden. Joey was 11 years old and a lot of help in the fields and the barn. Ruthie, 9 years old, was learning the womanly skills by helping her mother. She no longer was considered the keeper of the swing board. She could fry eggs and potatoes and make coffee. She could also put a mean patch on overall knees, and was looking forward to harvesting and canning for the winter. The Morrison farm was doing as well as some of their neighbors and better than others. Dag Brown came as often as he thought Old Prancer could make the trip, but he had responsibilities at home to take care of. Donald and Emily made a good thing of their union and were expecting a baby in two more months. Vern seemed to really enjoy all the activity around his home.

Donald announced at breakfast that he thought they would like to celebrate their approaching child. The cheapest thing they could do was to go into town and spend the evening at the free Concert in the Park. He would pick up the mail and a few supplies that they needed. They might even have lunch with the Dunsmores.

When they entered the Dry Goods Store, Floyd put on a big smile and said he and Clara had been expecting them and right at this minute, Clara was home preparing a roast beef dinner for tonight. Emily was happy with this idea as she thought she could just relax with another woman for a bit before they went out tonight.

Donald left her with Clara and went to the post office. Imogene Turner, the postmistress, greeted Donald with a little frown on her face, and said, "There was a man here inquiring about Emily yesterday." Red flags went up in Donald's world immediately. "What did he look like?" he asked. "Oh!" she said, "I guess he looked like your average run-of-the-mill hobo. He had a backpack and his clothes looked like they had a few hundred miles on them."

"What was his name?"

"He didn't say, but he knew she was from Wolf Creek, Illinois."

Donald's heart sunk into his boots. "Can you describe him? How tall was he? What color was his hair and eyes?" He knew Emily would want to know all these things.

"He was about as tall as you and his hair was mainly covered up by an old hat but I think it was dark and his eyes were brown. Seemed like an agreeable feller"

"What did you tell him about her?"

"As little as I could. But all he had to do is inquire at any of the stores here and he could find out anything he wanted to." By now, everyone in town knew the story of Emily and Harlan and Donald, and all privately agreed that it was more than likely that Harlan would never come back. A lot of people in these times were disconnected from their families.

Donald detested the idea of spoiling their celebration but he knew that Emily might never forgive him for withholding this information from her, even for a few hours. He returned to his grandparent's house and decided that Floyd and Clara might have some useful advice about the situation. When they sat down to supper, Clara sensed that something was wrong and said so. He told them exactly what was happening. Emily started crying and said, "How can I say that I don't want Harlan to come back? But this has been my worst nightmare since Donald and I decided to live together as man and wife." Donald reached over and put his hand over hers on the table and said, "Now, Sugar, we don't know who this is or what kind of a message he has. Let's not suppose the worst."

Floyd said, "I did see a stranger in town yesterday and I thought he might come into the store but he never did. I asked my boy, Johnny, when I came back from lunch and he said no, he had not come in, but he went to the hardware store and the Diner. I can make some discreet inquiries around town."

Emily was so upset that they decided not to go to the Park. Donald told Floyd if the man came back and he had a chance to talk to him, to send him on out to the farm. He could see nothing to be gained by hiding from him. They went home early and told Vern and the kids what they had learned. Joey told her later that night that he would be glad to see his dad, if it was him, but he knew it would be rough on everybody, especially with the baby coming. He said, "When we first knew Grandad, he told me and Ruthie that sometimes bad things happen to good people and there ain't nothing' to do but to put one foot in front of the other and keep carryin' on. So, Mom, you remember that. If it is Dad, we'll have to decide what to do about it. Not only you, but me and Ruthie, and Donald, too, and maybe even the baby."

Life around the farm went on as normal for two days. Donald tried to stay close to the house and when he had to be farther away, told Emily to ring the dinner bell and he would be there as soon as possible. Joey worked in the garden with Ruthie and his mother. Just before lunchtime on the second day, Old Spot, Donald's big black dog, started barking. Emily looked out at the road and there was a transient turning in their driveway. She turned to Ruthie and said, "Ring the bell! It's almost lunchtime anyway." She came out of the garden to meet him; uncertain if this was the man they had been waiting for. She knew right away that it wasn't Harlan, so she told Joey to show him where to clean up and she would start lunch.

He was washing himself and Joey had produced the signature pile of clean clothes for him to put on if his own clothes needed to be washed. However, he declined, saying that he had been to a house yesterday where the lady had washed his clothes for him. As he was finishing his ablutions, the men came from the field. Emily came out on the stoop and Donald looked at her questioningly. She shook her head slightly, and Donald went to greet the man.

Emily had made sandwiches and fried potatoes and sweet tea. The men sat down and as usual, silently went about eating. When the meal was winding down, Donald looked at the stranger whose name was 'Digger' and said, "Are you the feller that has been in town asking about Emily Jones?"

"Yep," said Digger, "Do you know her? I was told she was here, but the only woman I see is your wife."

There was a moment of silence and then Donald said, "My wife's name was Emily Jones until we entered into a common-law marriage. Her husband left for California four years ago and she never heard anything more from him."

Joey spoke up then, "Do you know anything about Harlan Jones? He was my father and we think something bad happened to him or he would have written to us."

Digger replied, "I do, son. I met up with him right after he left home and you are right about one thing. He fully intended to keep in touch with his family. We were both headed for California to find work and liked each other, so we decided to team up. We were hopping freights and sleeping at hobo camps. We got to be pretty good at evading the guards at railroads and were almost to the West Coast when it happened. We had given each other a piece of paper with family names and addresses on them, just in case of an accident. It happened and in a split second he was gone. I done as I had promised him and made my way back to Wolf Creek to find his family, but as you can see, it has taken me 4 years. I couldn't see where it would do anybody any good for me to go back and maybe be clubbed by the guards. Some of them were pretty mean. I went on to Californy and intended to write to you in Wolf Creek. I couldn't bring myself to do it so after I found out that Californy wasn't the Land of Opportunity it was supposed to be, I decided that I had to find you and tell you about it in person." Emily and the children were silent and he went on, "I know this is shocking to hear how he died but I have to tell it the way it is." Joey asked, "Is there more?" Digger continued, "Yes, when I came back East I headed for Wolf Creek. People there said that you had packed up and they thought you had headed for Virginny like two or three years ago. Just before I left there, I went to the post office and they said they had an address for you in Perryville, Kentucky. I started walking and when I got here, I had a deuce of a time trying to get any information from anybody. They didn't seem to want to tell me anything. Then I went into a Dry Goods Store and the old man there sang like a canary."

Donald said, "That is my grandfather, and I had told him if he saw you again to send you out here. It has been hard on Emily and the kids not knowing what happened to him."

Emily put in her two cents worth, "It has been hard on all of us since Donald and I entered into a common-law marriage. None of us knew exactly what would happen if he came back. We all thought that something had happened to him or he would have contacted us."

"Yes, ma'am, he certainly intended to," said Digger. "Now, if I could use your barn to get a little shut-eye, I'll be leavin'". Vern, aroused from his own thoughts, said, "I'm not goin' to the field this afternoon. Why don't you just set on the porch for a while, and leave after breakfast tomorrow? Emmy may think of somethin' else she wants to ask you." Emily cast a grateful look at Vern and nodded her head.

Digger agreed and he and Emily did talk some more. He suddenly remembered something and he picked up his duffel bag and began rummaging around in it. He unwrapped a small object from an old piece of newspaper and held it out to Emily. I was wearing Harlan's jacket when the accident happened and this was in his pocket. Do you recognize it?" The children had been out in the yard working where Joey could sort of keep an ear open to what was going on. He sensed now that something momentous had arisen. He went right to his mother to see what she was looking at. He pointed to a tiny mark scratched into the corner of an old harmonica, but before he could say anything, Ruthie let out a squeal. "It's Daddy's mouth organ. I know it is. He used to play it when I was sitting on his lap." Emily thanked him and went into the house. It was all she could do to keep the tears from spilling over. That night, Donald asked her if she felt better about things and she said, " I'm not sure what I feel. Part of me feels kind of empty. I want to cry for the way he died, but the other part of me is grateful to know something about him for sure. We still don't have enough proof to have him declared dead, but I feel that there is enough for us to go on with our lives."

Donald said, "Well, Sugar, if you feel like cryin'. you just go ahead and cry. I know you had good feelin's for him and he is your children's father." He stood there with his arms around her while she mourned for her first love.

Vern sat there in a thoughtful reverie for a few minutes. When Donald joined him on the porch their eyes met and Vern said, "I think we need to pay a visit to Mr. Digger. There is something he isn't telling us."

Digger was just settling into some fresh straw in the box stall for the night when the barn door opened and the two men stood there. They didn't appear to be menacing, but Digger got to his feet anyway. The shorter of the two, Digger thought his name was Vern, said, "I think you've got a little more to your story that we would like to hear. It seems to me that you stopped kinda' short at one point and switched directions."

"Yes, sir," said Digger, "I did. I didn't want to tell the lady how her man died. I got a cousin who was marked while he was still in the womb by a shock his mama received."

"Well, I don't know how much stock to put in an old wives' tale, but I guess I would rather err on the side of caution." Donald had contributed this bit of rhetoric to the conversation. "So how did he die? If we know, we can tell her some day."

"We were running to catch a freight car when his foot slipped and he went under the train. It was at Grant's Crossing, Wyoming on October 15, 1930. I saw the guards later with a burlap bag and some tongs, picking up pieces of something around the place he died. Maybe if things ever get better you can contact the authorities there and see if they know anything about him. Some of those police keep pretty good records of what was left. One told me that someday this nightmare is going to end and then people are going to want to find their loved ones." After a moment in deep thought, he said, "He was known around the hobo camps as 'Mr. Blues', because of his harmonica. He might have even had it written somewhere. He was right proud of the name."

He slept in the barn, ate a couple of good meals, and was gone by 10 o'clock the next morning with a bag of food stashed in his backpack.

Chapter 20

ODE TO A MULE

Thanksgiving was coming up and everybody was looking forward to Dag's annual visit, which had become a semi-annual visit since the appearance of Emily and the children. Emily played something on the pump organ every night after supper, but when Dag was present they had a more spirited celebration of music. It seemed almost as though they were at the County Fair and the calliope was to be found in the vacant lot right beside Dunsmore's Dry Goods. Emily cherished that old organ more than she could say.

Thus it was with a great deal of disappointment two days before Thanksgiving that she opened the letter Donald had delivered to her from the post office. It was from her father and was written in a surprisingly meticulous handwriting. Following is a series of letters to and from the household in Perryville.

November 15, 1934

Dearest Emily and all the rest,

I am very sorry to tell you that I cannot be with you this holiday. Something sad has happened. Old Prancer has took sick. Even if I had another way to get there, I could not leave my old friend by herself. I don't know what it is except maybe old age. She is just feeling puny and not up to making the trip. Maybe by spring she will have perked up and we can come to see you. Your babe should be born by then and I am fretfully waiting to hold it in my arms, as I never got to do this with Joey and Ruthie.

Love to all of you.
Daggett Brown

December 2, 1934

Dear Dad,

We are all so sorry to hear about Old Prancer and even more sorry that you were not with us to celebrate Thanksgiving. When we all did our 'thankfuls' before we ate dinner, the kids and I were most thankful for you being in our lives. This is not new as we put you at the head of the list every year, but I just wanted to remind you. Also on the list (for me) was Donald and the new baby. Vern was thankful for the fine crops we had this year. Joey and Ruthie are both thankful for Topsy who faithfully takes them to school every day. Joey cares for her like she was his baby. They are both doing well in school. Donald's arithmetic lessons at home have been highly praised by Mr. Powell, the teacher. Well, he praised their reading and writing skills, too, which I guess is due to me.

We are all quite excited about the coming of the new baby. We will name it Vernon if it is a boy and Eleanor Flora (for Eleanor Roosevelt and Donald's mother) if it is a girl. I hope you're not offended for not naming a boy after you. It is supposed to be born about the 20th of February. We found a box in the attic of Donald's baby clothes and I washed and pressed them and put them in the little chest of drawers that Donald and Vern made out in the woodshop. Donald brought in a large pan that they use in butchering hogs to use for the baby's bath and I cleaned it all up. More next time.

Love,
Emily

P.S. Donald says I forgot to tell about his thankfuls. I guess it embarrassed me. He is thankful for me and that I married him.

December 15, 1934

Well, Emmy-girl, I sure enjoyed your letter. Sure not much doubt about my thankfuls. I'm thankful for you, too. I am not offended about the name. Daggett is my name and it is a fine name for me but I would hate to saddle a little boy now with it. Vern and me have always been all right with each other, so there will be no hard feelings. Thanks for all the news about Thanksgiving, but you didn't tell me what you had to eat. Did Vern and Donald manage to shoot a wild turkey? Or did you have to fall back on one of the hens? Did any hoboes show up for dinner this year? I know you would include them if they came, on account of how you felt about Harlan. Vern always had a soft spot in his heart for them anyway. Old Prancer seems to be getting weaker and weaker. I don't know what to do for her. I have to coax her to get up to go to the water trough. Maybe I will try bringing a pail of water into the barn. I think the yellow curtains I put up in the barn cheer her up, though. I see her looking at them sometimes. I will not be able to come for Christmas this year either but have managed a few little presents. I guess they will wait until we can get together. I think about you all a lot. Tell Little Missy to write me a letter. She can do it. If she needs help, Joey can write some, too.

Dag Brown

December 26, 1934

Hello, Dag,

Just a short note to tell you about something I saw in Floyd's Dry Goods the other day. It is a new product made by the Watkins Company and it is called horse liniment. It can be taken internally or rubbed on the outside, whichever is fitting. The directions on the bottle say it is also good for rheumatism and headaches. Maybe if you can get into Gulchy Gap they would have some at the hardware store. It might put some ginger into Old Prancer. Emmy says to tell you that Donald and I both shot a wild turkey. As usual, Emmy did it up brown and it was mighty tasty. She put corn bread dressing in them and we had mashed potatoes, candied sweet taters, applesauce, and pumpkin and mincemeat pies. There were 2 transients that showed up at the gate early in the morning. I guess they didn't want to miss out.

As Ever, Vern

January 8, 1935

Dear Grandpa,

We are sorry about Old Prancer. She has been a faithful old mule. I like the way she made the bells jingle on the slay when we came to your house. When I'm not feeling good, Mama gives me a dose of sulfur-molasses and puts me to bed with a hot water bottle on my feet. I don't like it but she says it makes me feel better. There is a deep snow bank between home and the schoolhouse so Mama and Donald are teaching us until the snow melts. This letter was going to be from Joey, too. He doesn't like to write letters so he said he would do my chores 1 day if I would put his name on my letter, but Mama found out about it and said NO, he has to write his own letter. So this letter is not from Joey.

I love you, from Ruthie, your granddaughter

January 10,1935

Dear Grandpa,

Mom made me write my own letter so here it is. I have never written a letter before so don't know exactly how to do it. I will try. We have missed seeing you and Old Prancer this winter. I am sorry that she is sick. Are you giving her any medicine? Sometimes that helps. Be sure and make her drink a lot of water. Does she have a cold? Does she have a stomach ache? Donald says that he will come and get you in the truck any time you want to come. Our new baby will be here in 6 weeks, Mom says. I don't think about it much as I don't think I care much for babies. Mom says I will but I don't think so.

Your grandson, Joey Jones

January 20, 1935

Well, folks, the worst thing has happened. Old Prancer died day fore yesterday. I was with her and she tried to get up but even with me helpin' her she couldn't make it and she just lay down and give a gasp, give me a helpless look with her eyes and stopped breathing. I ain't ashamed of it. I just sat there and cried my heart out. I sat with her most all day singin' songs; she liked to have me sing. But this mornin' I had to call the 'dead wagon'. The man that owns the 'dead wagon' hauls away big animals, otherwise what would we do with them? An ordinary man can't handle something like that. I cried some more when they drove out of the driveway. I don't know how I can stay here by myself right now. If Donald wants to come get me to stay a few days for a visit, I would be obliged.

With Love, Dag

Chapter 21

A New Beginning

February 1, 1935

Uncle Dag,

If I am going to come for you before the baby comes it will have to be next weekend. You will need to be ready when I get there so we can come back in the same day. I would never forgive myself if I missed the birth of my first child. Emmy wants you here for the occasion, too. Bring enough to stay for a few weeks, as I don't know when we'll be able to bring you home.

Your nephew, Donald

As it turned out, Vern and Joey were the ones to drive to Gulchy Gap to bring Dag back for a visit. On the designated day, Emily was feeling under the weather and she didn't want Donald to be absent from home all day. The trip took them about two hours but it seemed much longer because the heater in the truck wasn't working. Their toes, nose, and fingertips were all on the edge of frostbite when they got there. Dag had a good fire going in the fireplace. The chickens and the cow had all been taken to the neighbors to be cared for and the old dog, Blackie, who was brown and white spotted, was going along. Vern and Dag hoisted the doghouse into the back of the truck and Blackie jumped into the truckbed and hunkered down into the new straw. The two men agreed that they would stop every 10 miles to see if Blackie was all right and if he was cold they would find room inside the truck for him. The only heat they had inside was body heat but it was better than nothing.

As they approached the end of the drive and prepared to turn onto the county road, Dag shouted, "Stop! Dang it, I forgot somethin'." He got out and ran for the barn. Vern couldn't imagine what he had in the barn that he needed to take with him, but he guessed that there was some kind of reasoning behind his actions. In a few minutes Dag came out of the barn carrying a large paper bag and put it behind the seat. He didn't offer an explanation and they didn't ask for one. It was just the way of Kentucky country folks.

They arrived in Perryville about 4 o'clock and everyone was glad to see them. Donald and Joey went right out to start chores and Ruthie was busy peeling potatoes for supper. When Emily went to the kitchen, Dag followed her and found her apron hanging behind the door. He put the apron on himself and bade Emily to sit in the chair and give instructions. He was determined not to make himself a burden to her. First she had him build up the fire in the cook stove. Then she sent him to the root cellar for some canned beef and canned corn. She and Ruthie had made a cake that afternoon, so there wasn't too much to do.

As supper wound down to an end, Ruthie turned to Dag, and said, "Well, Grandpa, are you going to play the organ and sing for us tonight?" Dag pretended to be thinking it over when in reality he was pleased as punch. "Well, I guess I could," he finally said, "Iff'n we get this supper mess cleaned up in a hurry." Thus the precedent was set for his whole visit. Life went on for the next two weeks with Dag picking up a lot of Emily's tasks so that she could rest. The two dogs, Spot and Blackie, had quickly formed an alliance and slept together, either in the doghouse or the barn. No one had figured out how the residence for the night was determined between the two of them, but they seemed to have some kind of signal known only to them.

In the early morning of February 20, 1935, a snowstorm hit the area around Perryville bringing with it sleet and slippery roads. Emily woke up before anyone else and when she got out of bed, she felt something wet on her feet. Her water had broken and labor probably wouldn't be far behind. Donald also arose quickly and was dispatched to bring Mrs. Berry, the midwife Emily had engaged to help her when the time came. He was also to alert Doc Pritchard in town who would come out later. Vern and Joey took care of the barn chores and Ruthie took care of the chickens. Mrs. Berry set the bedroom up with clean linens and a rubber sheet over the mattress. The air was heavy with excitement and expectation. Everyone was anxious to see this new little person. Everyone except Joey, that is, who still maintained that he was not interested in babies.

Emily's labor went on at a slow pace all day and Donald was beginning to look the worse for wear. The doctor arrived right after supper and got her out of bed and walking around a bit. He said that sometimes that would speed things up a bit. It seemed to work and about 8 o'clock the waiting troops in the kitchen heard a loud wail. Donald came out to get some warm water out of the reservoir on the stove and warm cloths that Mrs. Berry had put in the warming oven. He gave them the news that it was a boy and Emily was fine, then hurried back into the bedroom. He had kept a fire going in the fireplace all day so the bedroom was nice and cozy. A half hour later he came to the kitchen door and said, "Who would like to come in and welcome Vernon Daggett to our household?"

Ruthie jumped up with, "Mama said I could hold him first." All the rest of the entourage rose at once and moved toward the bedroom door. Ruthie sat in the rocking chair and Donald placed the warm little bundle in her arms. She wanted to see his fingers and toes so Donald helped her unwrap him to get to the desired parts. Vern called Donald's attention to Dag, who was standing there wringing his hands so Donald picked the babe up and placed him in Dag's arms. Dag stood there in a daze just staring at him. Tears were running down his cheeks. He handed the baby to Vern and hustled out the door and headed upstairs to his bedroom. "What's the matter with Dag?" Donald asked. "He's just a bit overwhelmed, same as I was the first time I saw you" Vern told him.

He had been watching Joey, the uninterested party. He was still trying to act like the new baby was of no interest to him but somehow; he seemed to be straining very hard to see what was going on. Donald noticed him at the same time and took his hand and led him to the rocking chair. Vern placed the baby in Joey's arms. Everyone had heard Joey's brags about not liking babies so they were all watching and holding their breath when Joey reached his finger toward the little boy's hand and he instinctively wrapped it around his big brothers finger and also his heart. A big smile spread across Joey's face and they all knew everything was going to be all right.

Vern slipped out of the room and went to find Dag. He was sitting on the edge of his bed and his face was red from rubbing at the tears. "I didn't mean to get so troubled, Vern, but I never thought I would get to hold my grandson in my arms. I just can't tell you the feeling after all those years of being alone."

He picked up the paper bag he had been holding and arose from the bed. Back in Emily's bedroom he took a little blue sweater from the bag and handed it to her. "Your mama knitted this for you afore you was born. I thought you might like to have it for Vernie." He waited for everybody to admire it and then reached into the bag again. "This here is from Old Prancer. Vernie won't never know what it's like to ride in the sleigh with Prancer making the sleigh bells jingle." He pulled out Prancer's old straw hat with ear holes cut in it. " I made this hat the first year I had that old mule cause I didn't want her to get sunstroke. I walked a good many miles behind the plow watchin' her rear end sway from side to side and her head bobbin' up and down with this old hat on. Sometimes, I'd even take a turn at wearin' it myself. Now, mind you, this ain't a play pretty. I thought maybe Donald could make a real nice frame to put this in and we could hang it on the wall in Vernie's bedroom. I plan on telling' that boy a passel of Old Prancer stories afore I get through with this life.

Nobody quite knew what to say so they all just stared at the hat. Thus was little Vernie hung with a unique monicker and gift, and at the same time an old friend of his grandfather's was immortalized.

Chapter 22

The Twins

Donald, true to the expectations about Old Prancer's hat, had made a display case about 15 by 12 by 3 inches to hang on the wall. He put his finest workmanship into it and it was truly something to behold. To top it off, he gave the old hat a thick coat of shellac before he anchored it into the frame with tiny brads. Dag was well pleased with it and when it was finished he decided it was time to go home. He had been visiting almost 2 months and was getting a little anxious about the state of his farm. He was going to miss the babe, whom he had held and rocked every day he had been there, but he had already figured out that he would beg rides, and hitchhike and maybe even procure another animal to ride- probably a horse-in order to visit the Morrisons.

It was a Tuesday morning in April 1935, and planting time was approaching. Dag had bargained with a neighbor who owned modern machinery to work up the land for him. He was out in the barn doing a last minute inspection of his crop seeds when he heard an automobile coming down the drive. It was a smooth sound, unlike any that he had heard before. Stepping to the barn door, he saw a late model Packard 8 Phaeton stop by the back porch. It was something to look at with a gray body, red wheels and spare tire cover, a speed goddess hood ornament, and a white roof. Two tall, slender men got out, reached in the back seat for some towels, and started wiping the dust and dirt off their automobile. They had black identical suits, shoes, and identical haircuts. That is, what hair there was. All they had was a white fringe around the sides and back of their scalp. Their movements and mannerisms began to make his scalp tingle. Who were they? Were they Revenuers? He had a little still back up on the mountain but he hadn't sold any 'shine' for ever so long. They looked and acted almost like twins. TWINS! That was it. This had to be his twin brothers, Garrett and Barrett. They had left home about the turn of the century and headed for Alaska. News of Alaska's Gold Strike in 1897 had incensed them and they were off to make their fortune in the gold mines. It looked like they may have found their fortune all right, if their dress and automobile were any indication.

As Dag approached the men, one of them looked up and a wide grin came across his face. "Brother Daggett," he said, "Barrett here! Garret there!" They shook hands and Dag inquired about where they had been and what they were doing here. It seems they had struck a small lode in the Alaska Gold Rush but mostly they had been working for the Pinkertons. They owned the automobile, their wardrobe of stylish clothes, and little else. Dag suspected they had some hidden bank accounts, but was too polite to ask. He sensed that they wanted him to admire the Packard so he put everything he had into it. He climbed into the driver's seat even though he knew 'from nothing' how to drive a car. Finally he said, "Why don't we go in the house and I will get something to eat." He truly was glad to see them even if it had been 35 years with scarcely any word of their whereabouts. He got a letter occasionally from Taggert or Claggett. They had taken their families and gone to Texas where they were ranchers. Bell was a laborer on the Titanic that went down in the North Sea in 1912. Maggie had married Angus McDonald, a farmer from Tipton County. They had 8 children last he knew. Agnes had married a college professor and moved to New York City.

They wanted to know if he had a bed for them tonight. He told them that they could sleep in the loft, and proceeded to prepare supper. They reminisced over the fact that Dag always had been able to set a good table and that hadn't changed. Dag reminded them how Maggie and Agnes kept his nose to the grindstone helping with the housework when he was a boy. Then Barrett remembered how Dag used to play the old pump organ and expressed his envy for that ability. Dag didn't mention Emily or Henrietta or anything else of a personal nature. He was a little uncertain about why they were here and decided to play his cards close to the chest. The next morning, he figured they would pack it in and leave. By 10 o'clock they had made no move to do so. When he mentioned that he was going to ride into town with a neighbor and get a few supplies, Garrett was adamant that they all go to town in the Packard. When they reached Gulchy Gap, the two men again got their towels out and wiped the car down. They had changed clothes and no longer wore the black suits. Dag was surprised to see that they did have some more suitable clothes for the country. Barrett insisted on buying the food supplies and by the time they ate supper that night, Dag decided that he was having a pretty good time with the twins and that they could be trusted.

He started opening up about his own life with the story of finding Emily and the children. Barrett asked, "How come she got lost in the first place?" Dag started the story:

"Do you remember that girl I was sweet on, Henrietta Morrison?" he asked.

"Yes," Garrett replied, "but we went away before anything happened."

"I married her and we had a little girl named Maybelle. She was the sweetest little thing with eyes just like mine and curly brown hair. I guess I wasn't a very satisfactory husband because after 3 years Henrietta run off with a drummer fellow that came through town selling tinware. The worst thing she did was to take little Maybelle away from me. I didn't know how to look for them-"

Barrett said, "Why didn't you call Pinkertons in? They probably could have found them."

Dag stared from one to the other and replied, "I didn't know nothin' about no Pinkertons and at first I thought she would come back." He continued with his story telling how he discovered Emily and the children at his brother-in-law's home 5 years ago when he went there to spend the Thanksgiving holiday. He told how the Andersons found a little 2-year-old girl on their doorstep one morning and kept her. He said at first he thought Henrietta had abandoned her but now that he has had a chance to think about it some, he thinks she wouldn't have done that willingly. Garrett silently contemplated all that was being said and finally opened up and started talking. He was telling Dag all about their work with Pinkerton's and some of the tools they had to work with. He said the Pinkerton's motto is 'The Eye That Never Sleeps'. He told him about the network of people around the country and the history of the company. He ended his dissertation by saying, " We'd like to talk to this woman you think is your daughter. Has she ever asked you for money? It sure seems far-fetched that she turns up on your brother-in-laws front porch 27 years after your wife took her away."

Dag said, "How do you account for the dresses and the doll? I had Henrietta's dress and the doll. Emily has the dress that she had on when the Anderson's found her and it was all the same cloth. She has a locket that she had on with a picture of me and Henrietta and a babe. She has the scar in the palm of her hand from when she cut herself on a piece of glass while she still lived with me. How can you argue with these facts? And she ain't never asked me for nothin'"

Barrett said, "Well, it sure sounds like you're onto something, but we would still need to talk to her and see all this evidence." Dag allowed as how he could understand that and asked them how long they would be staying. The twins looked at each other and Garrett signaled for Barrett to go ahead and talk; "The truth is that we're tired of working and want to retire. We have been away from family for many years and would sort of like to settle near some of them. We want to visit Maggie and Agatha. We already been to see Tag and Clag. Texas didn't appeal to us and neither did the uproar that 2 bunches of kids makes." Dag began to grin and said, "You won't do much better with Maggie, then, she has 8." On second thought he said, "If I remember her right, her kids are probably pretty well behaved. Can I suppose you might want to live near me?" "Maybe- maybe not" answered Garrett with a grin of his own.

That night, Barrett and Garrett discussed Emily and Henrietta and decided that they would look into the situation while they still had the Pinkertons behind them. In the morning they told Dag about their decision and he decided that he had 2 weeks before spring planting would begin. By 1 o' clock they were on their way to Perryville.

Donald and Vern were out in the barn examining their tools and seeds in preparation for spring planting. They heard the Packard just before it turned into the driveway. They were speechless. Not only had they never seen such a sight in this part of the country, they didn't even know Packards existed. As they stood agog outside the barn door with their mouths hanging open, the two men in the front seat dressed in black suits and ties reached for their towels and started the ritual of cleaning the auto. Not until Dag started for the barn did they even see him. Why watch for a sparrow when there was a Bird of Paradise performing? Only then did they walk toward the house to meet their guests. Emily and the children had already come out of the house and Joey was examining the machine from a distance. Dag introduced them all around and noted that their nicknames were Garr and Bear. Emily noticed that they were both giving her the Eagle eye.

Since it was not quite time to start supper, they all went into the parlor. Dag inquired about little Vernie and was told to get him out of his crib in the kitchen. He brought the baby in and told the brothers about him. All conversation came to a halt as they gazed at the tiny bundle. Bear said, "You have to forgive us for ogling but we never been this close to a babe before, at least not for 45 years."

Garr spoke up, "I'd like to hold onto him if it's all right." He sat down in the rocking chair and gazed into the little fellow's face as though he was getting very close to finding someone for Pinkertons. Bear said, in a plaintive voice, "Now, don't be hoggin' that babe, Garr, I'd like to hold him, too. "Garr reluctantly gave the baby over to his brother. It was the start of an ongoing love affair.

Dag restarted the conversation by saying, "Ya won't ever believe the crazy ride I had over here. It only took us a little over an hour. Old Prancer must be turnin' over in her grave. Sometimes the sights along the road was just a blur." Joey spoke up excitedly, "Uncle Barrett, will you take me for a ride in your automobile?" Barrett answered, "Yes sir, young man, we'll do that, in fact, we'll take all of you for a ride tomorrow morning. That is, if your folks will be good enough to let us sleep in the barn."

Joey came right back with the answer, "No need for that. The two of you can have my bed. I'll sleep down here on the horsehair sofa." The twins looked at Emily for confirmation and when she nodded, they both smiled broadly. The next hour was spent in getting acquainted and finally Dag said to Emily, "Ain't it about time fer me to get some things out of the root cellar fer supper?" Emily and Ruthie stood to go to the kitchen and Emily said to Dag, "You know what to get. I made apple pies this morning so we have some dessert. Get meat and vegetables and it won't take long."

After supper was over, everyone retired to their bedrooms in anticipation of tomorrow. Donald and Joey were imagining what it would be like to drive such a magnificent machine. Vern and Dag were reaching back into their memories before 'Hard Times' at other magnificent machines they had seen. Emily was wondering what life would have been like as a child if these two spectacular men had been in it. Ruthie was wondering what it would be like to be the Goddess of Speed hood ornament. Garr and Bear were discussing Emily in the confines of Joey's bedroom. "What do you think about her, Bear?

"Whatever else can be said, she seems to be true. I like her."

She does have Dag's eyes, and so do the kids."

"Can't tell about the babe. He looks a whole lot like his daddy."

"We need to spend some time with her and get her story from her own lips."

"Yeah, we need to go at this like it was an authentic Pinkerton case."

"She can sure play that old pump organ. Remember how Ma taught Dag to play that old organ in the parlor when we was younguns. I wonder if he still plays it." Bear indicated that he had finished the conversation and wanted to go to sleep.

Chapter 23

THE PINKERTONS GET TO WORK

Emily and Dag had put together the most marvelous breakfast the twins had eaten in a long time. They were finding this visit to be thoroughly enjoyable. In fact, it was the most satisfactory of any they had experienced with their brothers and sisters so far. They had talked with Donald out in the barn this morning about the investigation they were planning and he was bubbling over with enthusiasm. He was all for finding out about Emily's mother but also he told them about Harlan and asked if they could uncover anything about him.

As breakfast came to an end, Donald announced that Ruthie and Dag should take care of the kitchen and little Vernie as the Uncles wanted to talk to their mother in private. Emily looked suspiciously at the two men, and Bear said, "We think we can find out what happened to your mother, but we need to have your say about it." Garr added, "And your husband, too." Emily was stunned. The Andersons had given her a good life but they had both died young in the flu epidemic of 1919. She had never had too much time to wonder about her true heritage, and everything that was coming her way now seemed like a gift.

The three went into the parlor and as Donald shut the door behind them, Bear said, "We have decided to conduct this like a regular Pinkerton investigation, as that is the way we know how to do it." Garr took up the discussion, " We'd like you to tell us everything you remember right from the time you went to live with the Athertons along with any items you may have from the past. We'll get to your husband later. Right now we want to focus on you"

"The Andersons," she corrected. She left to collect all the treasures she had garnered both from her childhood and Harlan. She returned shortly with a large shoebox and started telling them her story. They had already heard Dag's story and made notes in their notebook. She showed them the dress and locket she had on when the Andersons found her on their doorstep. Garr said, "Sure as shootin', that looks like brother Dag there in that ornament. She also showed them Henrietta's dress and the doll dressed in the same material. She showed them the scar on the palm of her hand that Dag had told them about. She also showed them the tiny mole behind her right ear that was identical to one Dag had in the same place. Bear had been busy with a sketchbook all the time she had been talking. Vern and Dag both thought the drummer's name was Silas Allbright or something similar, but maybe it was a false name. Vern, although it pained him mightily, had admitted that his sister had always been a bit flighty. And, as far as Emily knew, the Andersons were an old established family in Wolf Creek, Illinois and had never lived anywhere else. They had no other children at the time that Emily came to them. Jane was born 2 years later and the sisters had always enjoyed a good understanding. Frank and Mary Anderson had opened the front door of their home on the morning of September 2, 1904 to find the little girl sitting on the steps with a small bag of belongings and a note pinned to her dress that said, "I can't take care of her no longer. Please be good to her." She produced the note from her box of mementoes. Mary Anderson had done all she could to keep the unknown little girl from disappearing completely. They figured she was about 2 years old and gave her that date for her birthday. Dag had told them that her birthday was March 24, 1902. The Andersons were in their 30's and had never been able to start a family, so this little girl was a gift from heaven. As often happened, once they relaxed about a family, Mary had discovered that she was with child. Then Emily told them about her first meeting with Dag and how she had felt a connection with him from his very first visit. She readily admitted that she wanted this to be true, even though her situation in life as Donald's wife was pretty stable now.

Bear then asked her, "What about your husband, Harry?" "Harlan Jones" she corrected once again. A hobo named Digger stopped by in June of '34 and told us that he and Harlan had been partners in trying to get to the Land of Opportunity."

Ah, yes," said Garr, "California"

"Yes," replied Emily, "That's where he struck out for the last time I saw him. He honestly thought he was making a better life for me and the children." Bear signaled for her to continue.

"Digger said that they were in Grant's Crossing, Wyoming, on October 15, 1930 trying to hop a freight car, when a couple of guards started chasing them. Harlan's foot slipped and he went down under the train. Digger didn't stop because some of those guards were pretty brutal with their nightsticks. Digger had on Harlan's jacket at the time and this was in the pocket." She produced the harmonica from her treasure trove with the initials HJ scratched into one corner. "Ruthie swears this is Harlan's harmonica. She sat on his lap many evenings while he played it. She says she watched him scratch his initials in it before he left home."

Garr had been busy taking notes on everything she said and now started to close his book. "Wait," she cried, "Digger said that hardly any of the hoboes used their real names and Harlan was known as 'Mr. Blues' in the hobo camps. He also said that the police chief in this particular town was quite thorough about keeping information on bodies they buried. He said that someday when the bad times were over, people were going to be looking for their loved ones." Garr responded then, "Yes, quite a few authorities have felt that way."

The men arose, signaling that the interview was over. Lunch had not been started yet and Bear announced that there was no need, because they were all going for a ride to town and would have lunch there at the Diner. Ruthie wanted to know if she should put on her Sunday dress and Garr told her that they would be wearing their black suits and bowler hats so he thought it would be sort of nice if they all dressed up. The men, including Joey, all looked a little bewildered at this bit of information. However, looking at Emily and Ruthie's faces, they all went to their rooms without protest and changed into their Sunday clothes.

Joey sat in the middle of the front seat. Donald, Vern, and Dag sat in the back seat with little Vernie. Emily and Ruthie sat on the jump seats that pulled down from the sides in the back. Bear had put fresh wildflowers in the little vases mounted on the doorposts on each side of the interior. Joey was having the time of his life especially when Garr let him squeeze the Klaxon Horn mounted to the right of the steering wheel. When they had parked outside the Hotel, Bear said, "We decided to come here instead of the Diner seein' as how you were all dressed up so nice. Now, you can order anything you want, Garr and me will pay the bill. And later this afternoon we'll go over to the Sweet Shoppe and get some ice cream." There were moans of delight from the gathering as ice cream had been around for a while, but not around the Morrison household. True to form, the twins produced their towels and started wiping the dust off their vehicle. Joey grabbed a towel and proceeded to help them. The afternoon progressed as planned and the next morning the twins departed for Wolf Creek to start their mission.

Chapter 24

LET THERE BE LIGHT!

It was 1936 and everyone in town was all abuzz about this new program called the REA. The Rural Electrification Association was to bring electricity to the farms in the country. President Roosevelt had come into office in 1932 and in the 4 years since, his New Deal program had started to set the country on its feet, or so it seemed. Vern did allow as how things seemed to be better. All those damn fools that had killed themselves after the Crash were gone and never would see how there could maybe be better times in the future.

There was the Tennessee Valley Authority, which was just in the first stages. It was building dams throughout Tennessee to provide waterpower for hydroelectric plants. They were supposed to make electricity available to the people in the Southeast part of the country, which had been more or less deprived since the War Between the States. The Rural Electrification Act would bring prosperity to farmers throughout the land.

The Citizen's Conservation Corps was planting trees and restoring the forests. The end result of all these programs was that they provided employment for thousands of people. Donald and Vern spent many hours over the supper table discussing the possibility of having light in their home and barn. It wouldn't only be light; it would be heat, muscle power, and many things to make life easier for the farmer. Ruthie said, "Do you mean that Mama and me wouldn't have to do our mending by lamplight?" Donald answered her, "That's what I mean, Tadpole, it also means that Pop and me and Joey wouldn't have to use the lantern to do our chores in the barn in the winter. If we had one of these new milking machines in this booklet the government sent us, we could buy more cows and have a bigger milk check. We could use electricity to heat the water for baths and washing clothes. We could have one of these drop cords; they call 'em, with an Edison bulb that screws into it in each room. Some of them have a pull chain and if you pay enough money you can get a switch on the wall to turn the light on." He stopped to catch his breath and Joey took up the cause, "There is a thing here you put up on the wall and it's called an outlet. Then you buy a flatiron with a cord on it that you plug into the outlet and it makes the flatiron get hot. You wouldn't have to heat your old sadirons on the cook stove any more, Mom." Emily started laughing, "When are we going to get all the money to buy these things? Is President Roosevelt going to be sending us a check in the mail?" Without hesitation, Joey said, "Things are getting better, Mom, we'll have the money to buy things to make life easier some day. The president says we are supposed to read all these papers and decide what kind of fixtures we want and how many, so that when the electricity comes through here, we can tell the workmen what we want." The adults were all looking at Joey as though he had grown an extra head. They had no idea that he had been paying attention to all the talk.

On the first of February 1936, Vern received a letter from Apex Construction Company that they would be starting to string an electric line through 40 miles of Kentucky and it would go right past the Morrison place. A crew to wire houses and barns would follow right behind them. There was a new catalog included in the correspondence so that the homeowners could be ready to tell the crew boss what they wanted. Prices and loan packages were well defined and the adults started spending their evenings poring over the catalogs and forms to fill out. They decided that the drop cords would do in all of the rooms except the parlor. Emily wasn't insisting but the men could see that she wanted something a little nicer in there. She picked out a small chandelier with four arms on it with an Edison bulb that screwed into the openings. The choices were all very conservative. Later, out in the barn, the two men were discussing their choices when Donald said, "You know, Pop, Emmy doesn't ask for much and look at all that she gives us. Do you think maybe we could upgrade those fixtures we chose for the house? After all, we're having wall switches put in the barn." Vern replied, "I thought of that when we were talking about it, but I knew we would get nothing but objections from her. Maybe you and I can sort of change the orders a bit and surprise her. I was thinking she might be able to use one of those electric flatirons Joey was telling about, too. I been tossing around in my mind if we could afford a washing machine. There was one in the catalog that even had an electric wringer on it and it was only $15 on this program. We are getting one of those small milking machines for us, you know" "How does Joey know about all that stuff?" Donald asked. Vern answered, "I suspect Joey knows more about a lot of things than we think. He is pretty excited about this electricity thing. My feeling is that it is going to turn our lives almost 180 degrees."

The work started 20 miles east of them right on schedule at the end of January and progressed toward them at an alarming rate of speed. By July 1st the poles were all in to string the wire and on August 1st the wiring crew appeared at the door ready to start on the house and the barn. It took about two weeks to wire the barn. One morning, Emily saw a delivery truck turn in the drive. One of the men came to the door and asked her where she wanted the delivery they had. When she told him they could put it in the barn, he raised his eyebrows. "Well, Ma'am, I really don't want to put all this in the barn. You got a bit of money tied up in this shipment. Come on out and take a look." Emily followed him out to the truck. "I don't remember ordering all this stuff," she said. There was a washing machine, a flatiron, a milking machine, and several large boxes of light fixtures. She said, "I'll call Donald and you can talk about it with him." She hurried to the end of the porch and rang the dinner bell. Out in the field, the men heard the dinner bell and for just a few seconds a look of alarm passed over their faces. Then Vern said, "Oh, I saw a delivery truck go by on the road a few minutes ago. I'll bet our light fixtures are here." When they arrived at the house, Emily was in a dither. She met them on the porch and said, "I think they sent us the wrong order. I don't remember ordering all this stuff." Donald took one look and said, "This is what we ordered, isn't it, Pop?" Vern confirmed that it was and told them to take the milking machine to the barn and put the rest of it in the dining room. By the time it was all unloaded, Emily was inspecting the washing machine with a dazed look on her face. Vern told her, "What with all the work you have to do with the babe and all, we thought you deserved a little extra. We would have got this for Flora." Emily didn't hardly know whether she could speak without bursting into tears but finally she murmured, "Th-thank you!" and turned toward the kitchen.

By the last of October the work was finished. The new ceiling light fixtures were in and there was one outlet in each room, including the washroom-pantry. The electricity was due to be turned on November 2. About 7 PM on that day, three men in suits came to the door and said they had some papers for Vern to sign after the ceremony. The ceremony, of course, was to turn on the first light in the house. With them they brought a bottle of fine wine (so they said) to toast a new life for the Morrisons. One of them gave a little speech, one served the wine, and one laid the papers for Vern to sign on the table. Then #1 asked Emily to step to the switch and turn the first light on. When light burst out of the ceiling, everyone stood there in awe. Ruthie and Joey ran from room to room turning on all the lights in the house.

The men left and Donald said, "I want to see what the house looks like from the outside." Everyone followed him out to the barn where they could all view the house and admire all the light. A few weeks later the lights went out while they were eating supper. Ruthie went to all the rooms trying the light switches and finally gave up. They started lighting lamps to use until they went to bed. The household settled down and was soon asleep. At 3:10 AM every light in the house came on and there were a couple of screams from Ruthie's room Everyone was up and milling around to see what was the matter, when Emily and Donald started laughing. They were to learn that power failure was to be a common occurrence in the future. They also learned to make sure all the switches were turned off before they went to bed.

Chapter 25

VERN - 1937

Vern sat on a stump out in the woods in the back 30 acres, holding the shotgun ready in case he saw a wild turkey. He was mindlessly pondering his life. It had been a pretty satisfactory life. A lot of good things had come his way. He had had a feeling of doom for several months before the stock market crashed in 1929, so he had taken his savings out in the cornfield by an old tree stump and buried them. Donald knew where the 2-quart jar was buried just in case something happened to him. Dag had done the same thing, but he had told Vern where his was buried because he didn't have anyone else to tell.

Oh, he was not a rich banker but he hadn't lost his shirt when the Stock Market collapsed in '29. The farm that had been in his family for a hundred years was pretty secure and was feeding his present family well. There was even enough food stored away that he had loaded up 3 bushels of produce and taken it to the Widow Carpenter when Ruthie had come home from school and said that little Billy Carpenter didn't have any lunch, and she had shared hers with him. He had a 2-year-old grandson who was the apple of his eye. The sun was shining and the air was crisp. Yes, all was well in Vern's world this November morning.

Thanksgiving would be in two more days and he wanted to reap some of the provender from the woods for Thanksgiving dinner. He reflected that it was time somebody taught Joey to hunt, but Donald had a job in the barn that he needed some help with this morning. Besides, Joey needed more target practice before he could carry a gun in the woods. Just then, he heard a turkey call from somewhere to the right, and decided that he was not going to see any game where he was sitting. Picking his way through the woods as quietly as he could, he came to a fence dividing his property from his neighbor's. He was on good terms with his neighbors and was sure they wouldn't mind if he trespassed a little bit. Leaning his shotgun carefully against the fence post, he proceeded to climb over the fence. The post was loose in the ground, which should have been a warning. It wobbled ever so slightly, but it was enough to make the gun start to slide. The trigger caught on a protrusion from the post and the gun discharged. Vern had his left hand on top of the post directly in the line of fire. A white-hot pain shot through his arm and he fell back onto the ground. Lifting his left arm up, he saw a bloody mess where his hand should be. He couldn't tell if it had hit an artery or not but it was bleeding profusely. He knew that if he passed out, he would likely bleed to death right there in the woods. Pulling a fairly clean red bandana handkerchief from his pocket, he managed to make a tourniquet around his forearm and tie it tightly using his teeth. Knowing that he still needed help, he fired the remaining shot in his double-barreled shotgun. He fired 8 more shots in quick succession by reloading the gun as fast as he could manage. With his ammunition diminishing, all he could do now was wait and hope that Donald had heard the message. He was still bleeding but he thought not quite so fast. However, as he began to feel faint, he knew he needed help quickly. He had saved four more shells for when he heard them in the woods.

Donald and Joey heard the first shot and Donald grinned and said, "What do you want to bet that is our Thanksgiving dinner," and he smacked his lips as though he could already taste it. The second shot, he allowed was the second turkey. It startled him when he heard the successive shots. They seemed to be coming from the East where the woods were shared with the neighbor, Clare Willis. Suddenly, he was galvanized into action. "Come on, Joey, Pop's in trouble." He ran to the back door, shouting to Emily, " Joey and I are going to drive back to the woods and try to find Pop. I think he is in trouble. Grabbing some quilts and sheets out of the bedroom and taking a gun and some ammunition, he told her on the run what had happened. He took the time to fire off one shot and hoped that Vern would get the message that they had heard him and were on the way.

In the truck, he said to Joey, "From the sound of the shots, I think we can reach him faster by going on the back road. I brought the gun so he can hear me fire it and maybe we can find him quicker." Joey nodded wisely as though he had been doing this all his life.

Donald parked the truck where the woods bordered the back road, got out and promptly fired a shot. To his surprise an answering shot resounded from the woods close at hand. Following his instinct as to where the shot had come from, he started toward where he thought they might find Vern. Stopping every 200 feet or so to fire another shot, to which an answering shot came back each time, it didn't take long to find him, but when they saw the bloody mess that was once his hand, Donald knew they had better get him to the doctor in a hurry. He loosened the bandana and then tightened it again. Making sure that there were no shells in either gun, he handed them to Joey and picked his father up to carry him. He instructed Joey to run ahead and spread a quilt on the truck bed. When he had laid Vern on it and covered him as gently as he could, he told Joey to get in the back beside him. He said he would drive as carefully as he could but they needed to get to town fast. The latter was for Vern's benefit as he had managed to retain consciousness through the whole ordeal. It was a rough go, however and by the time they reached Doc Pritchard's house, Vern had passed out cold. Later, when Emily asked him how he managed to carry Vern out of the woods, Donald was at a loss as to what to tell her. The two men were a pretty close match for size and weight, except that Donald was about an inch and a half taller. Maybe it was enough of an advantage.

He didn't even bother to take Vern into the doctor's house. He just ran into the office shouting and Doc came right out to the truck. One look at the hand and he said, "I'll do a little emergency work on this hand and then you had better head right for Butterfield and the hospital as fast as you can. Who put the tourniquet on? The hand is in times gone by, but it probably saved his life. I'll send Buck from the garage out to your place to tell Emily so she won't fret." In less than 15 minutes, the Morrisons were on their way to Butterfield, a larger population, and a good hospital.

There was a good surgeon on duty that morning and he took Vern right into the operating room where he proceeded to remove the useless hand and make a good clean stump on his wrist. The operation took 3 hours and Donald and Joey had made a quick 30 mile trip home to leave Joey and for Donald to pick up a razor and clean clothes in case he had to stay overnight. By the time they had arrived at home, Emily and Ruthie had started the barn chores with little Vernie in the box stall with a toy where he would be out of harm's way. After he had told Emily about the events of the day, He quickly took a bath and put on clean clothes and sat down to an early supper, preparatory to returning to the hospital. There were more questions at the supper table but for the most part, everybody except Donald was somewhat subdued and ready to call it a day.

Donald arrived back at the hospital to find Vern conscious but somewhat sedated with morphine, and wanting to talk. "You all right, Pop?" Donald wanted to know.

Vern answered, "Yeah, but I wish they would quit moving my bed around. Danged painters want to work all night. I tried to stay awake to see 'em do the painting but I couldn't catch 'em."

"Looks the same as it did this morning to me," Donald told him.

"Well, it ain't," Vern said, "It was green this morning and now it's purple."

Donald changed the subject. "Pop, I want to talk about what happened to you this morning."

Vern began to cry. "So you can scold me, son? All the times I nattered at you about bein' careful with a gun, now it's your turn, I guess."

"It isn't ever going to be my turn to scold you for anything, Pop. I just want to know what happened," said Donald gently.

In little more than a whisper, Vern said to him, "I don't know if I can rightly tell you. I heard some turkey's over on Willis' side of the woods and I was climbing the fence. The next thing I knew, I was layin' on the ground and there was a bloody mess on the end of my arm. I knew if I didn't get help quick, I'd probably pass out and bleed to death. I can't thank you enough for readin' my gunshots so quick, son."

"You did just the right thing, Pop. The minute I heard all those shots I knew you were in trouble." Even as he spoke, Vern's body relaxed and he was asleep. Donald stayed with him all night as his sleep was very restless and once he woke up and told Donald that the nurse with the perpetual scowl had been giving his clothes to transients out of the back door. "Am I already dead and you just aren't telling me?" he asked. Donald knew that the morphine was making him hallucinate.

While he was sleeping, the day nurse came in and told Donald that they would be changing the dressings on Vern's arm in about 15 minutes and she would like Donald to watch because they would have to be changed every day when he went home. She gave him a gown, cap, and mask to put on. He came out of the bathroom just as the nurse came back with fresh bandages. She told him that Vern probably would stay about a week and he should go down to the cashier's office to make arrangements for payment. She also said that Emily should come in a couple of times to learn how to change the bandages and danger signals to look for. Memories of his mother's last days filled him with remorse. Maybe if they had known what to look for, she could have been saved. He watched the nurse zealously and asked questions about the wound.

Emily readily agreed to do her part and the next morning found her at Vern's bedside all decked out in hospital gear. He was lamenting to her the fact that he was not going to be very useful any more. She waited until he had spent himself, and then she said, " That is absolutely not true, Pop. You will not be dead weight on the rest of us. There are things you can still do. You just have to figure out what they are. I know you don't want to be relegated to the scrap heap, but some of the things that I need help with in the house are very important to the family's well-being. Donald and I were talking about this last night and he has things in the farm work that you can do. Some times life rises up and kicks us in the gut and we can't figure out why. We just have to get up and work out what it is that we <u>can</u> do. At least, nobody fell into any farm machinery and got themselves chewed up." She was silent for a few minutes, and then said, "Donald has been talking to people in town and some have told him some interesting things about artificial limbs. The wooden peg leg that old soldiers of the Confederacy wore is a thing of the past. I'm sure he will find out the best thing for us to do about your hand."

Vern heaved a deep sigh and said, "That's what I like about you, Emily, you always seem to be able to see things from a different viewpoint. Now, what about Dag? Does he know what is going on?"

"Yes," she said, "Donald went on over to Gulchy Gap day before yesterday. He wants to come and stay for a while to help Donald out until you get better. I'm supposed to drive over and pick him up after I leave here today." "Good," replied Vern, "He's a first-rate man to have on your side when times are troubled."

Emily watched the procedure of caring for Vern's injury carefully and then left to pick her father up and take him home with her. When she turned in the drive, Dag was sitting on the front porch with a duffle bag beside him. He had arranged for the neighbor boy down the road to take care of his cow and the dozen chickens scratching around the yard in exchange for the milk and eggs they would produce. He went to the old sedan to meet her and gave her a large hug. Only in the last year or so had he worked up enough nerve to hug her, but he liked to do it, he sure did. They departed for the farm and she filled him in on everything on the way home.

Chapter 26

THE PINKERTON'S RETURN

O n December 3, 1937, Donald arrived in Butterfield at the hospital at 10 o'clock in the morning. To him, it was a red-letter day, to be able to bring his father home after such a distressing accident. Vern was still uncertain as to how much he would be able to contribute to the good of the household, but after the bolstering talks Emily and Donald had given him, he was determined to make the best of a bad situation. Emily had suggested that they put off the Thanksgiving dinner until Vern was home and life wasn't quite so hectic. Day after tomorrow was the chosen day. A man from Bosker Turkey Farm in Dawsonville had visited them one morning with a Tom turkey for Thanksgiving dinner and a box with 3 turkey chicks in it. He said he didn't know if they were hens or toms but when they found out they could contact the farm if they needed a rooster. This would be the start of a small brood of Thanksgiving dinners for the future.

Dag and Joey had just finished the morning chores when the Buick sedan turned in the drive. Emily's old Ford had gone the way of all good things last year and Donald had managed to buy the old Buick for a song. Yes, times were slightly better than they had been.

Emily was preparing the turkey for the oven when she heard a car approaching the house. Looking up from her work, she saw a red and white Packard 8 phaeton out by the back porch. The twins had returned and, as usual were wiping down the automobile with towels from the back seat. They had been gone for almost 6 months and Emily was very excited about the possibility of learning something about her mother. Dag came out of the bedroom with Vern hanging onto his arm and in nothing flat everybody had gathered in the kitchen to greet the newcomers. Emily made a pot of coffee and they were all sitting around the kitchen table. Bear and Garr were thoroughly fascinated and, at the same time horrified by Vern's story. They both wanted to see the wound and Emily told them she would be dressing it with fresh bandages tomorrow and they would have to wait. They declared Donald and Joey heroes and goaded everybody into giving them an accolade with clapping of hands, whistles, and hooting.

Then they got down to the business at hand. Garr told about the trip to New York to see Agnes and her husband John Marston. They enjoyed a week there during which Agnes invited her son, Ted and his wife Trudy over to meet the brothers. Bear related their visit to Maggie and Angus' farm farther South in Georgia and meeting most of their 8 offspring. All of the brothers and sisters were happy to hear about Dag and the Morrisons and sent their regards.

Then Bear took a notebook from a brief case he had brought in with him and opened it up. He started by talking about their visit to Wolf Creek, Illinois. The Andersons were no longer alive but they had gone to the courthouse and perused the official records for a month surrounding the date that Emily said she was left on the Anderson doorstep. They interviewed the doctor who was a young man at that time and they could find no record of Henrietta's death or anyone who could give them any information. They were about to give up when the sheriff suggested that they retrace the route that the trio may have taken to get to Wolf Creek. They went back east about 10 miles to Scullybone and started with the sheriff's office. The lawmen there were all younger but Sheriff Terpin told them where they could find Joe Bob Gleason, the retired sheriff who would have been there at the time they were investigating. They drove out east of town and found him sitting in a rocking chair on his front porch. He was happy to have the company and turned out to be quite chatty. Much to their surprise, he fell right into the conversation about Henrietta. She had become ill with pneumonia in Nelly Cousin's boarding house. Her man seemed to be anxious to be moving on. The household had awakened one morning to find him gone and he had taken the child with him. Her sickness had worsened and she died during that day. All that Nelly knew about her was that her name was Henrietta. The town had buried her in the 'poor farm' section of the cemetery and put a small metal marker into the ground. Nobody knew where the 'drummer fellow' and the little girl went. They all assumed that she was his daughter. Joe Bob said that her name was Mable or something like that. He offered to go to the cemetery with them and show them where she was buried. Bear had taken a picture of the marker with his Super Brownie Camera. When the boys had finished their story Dag, Vern, and Emily all had tears in their eyes. Dag said, "I sure feel like a rotten apple. All these years I thought she was alive and happy with her fellow. Then when I found Emmy, I thought Henrietta deserted her. I guess I sort of did her a wrong."

Garr took up the story of their trip to Wyoming to check Harlan out. When they got to Grant's Crossing they went directly to the courthouse again and almost immediately found a record of the death of a transient who was called Mr. Blues by his fellow hoboes. The sheriff happened to be the one who had been in office when Harlan died and he was willing to talk about it. "He was pretty well chewed up by falling under the train but I went out personally and picked up the pieces. I went out to the hobo camp and they called him Mr. Blues. I didn't know his rightful name so I put that on his marker in the charity section of the cemetery." He told them how to get to the cemetery and they left. Garr then delved into the briefcase and came up with another picture of the marker on Harlan's grave and the death certificate for Mr. Blues. Joey took it and looked at it for a long time, but there were no tears. They had each shed their tears in private.

The next morning the twins asked Dag to drive over to Duncan Falls with them, about 20 miles away. A bit puzzled, he ran his mind over what he was going to do today. Nonetheless, he agreed and they left in mid-morning. They just enjoyed the scenery as none of them had ever been here before. They said there was an attorney there they wanted to see about something. After the session with him was over, Garr said, "Let's go to the hotel and eat some lunch. We've got something we want to talk over with you." They had ordered when Dag said, "Let's have it. Curiosity killed the cat, you know." Bear said, "Garr and I have talked over where we want to settle down in our retirement. We like this country and we like your people." Bear joined in, "We'd like to buy your place, or maybe just build a house of our own down the road a piece from yours. We saw something out in Wisconsin that set our nerves a jinglin' " It was a Sears Roebuck house that you could order from a catalog. The company sends it by rail to the nearest depot and we would have to transport it from there. They said that sometimes the train would even stop out in the country nearest to the building site as a special favor. Every piece is cut and marked so we think we could put it together ourselves. We could get one we liked real well for $800." Garr said, "We could even leave the log cabin as it is in case you wanted to come back to visit or even to live."

"Well, now," Dag said, "I ain't really been thinkin' about sellin' my place. But now that I think on it, things is workin' out pretty well with the Morrisons and I sure like bein' around Emmy and the younguns so much." As an afterthought he added, "I don't rightly know what Donald would do without an extra pair of hands. Did I tell you he has even showed me how to me to drive the tractor?"

As far as the boys knew, Dag had always been extremely opposed to combustible machines. Old Prancer had been good enough for him. They looked at each other and Bear gave a hardly noticeable nod of his head. Garr, who was driving, slowed the car and pulled over to the side of the road. "What's the matter? asked Dag, to which Garr replied, "You're going to learn to drive this car right now." With an astounded look on his face, Dag climbed into the driver's seat. With a fifteen-minute crash course in driving the Packard, they started out. Bear sat beside him and had him start and stop twice to give him practice, each time going over the items on the dashboard and their purpose.

An hour later, Emily was outside sweeping the porch when the trio turned into the drive. She squinted her eyes against the afternoon sun and to her amazement, saw that Dag was driving the twins auto. She ran to the end of the porch and rang the dinner bell. Vern came out of the house, followed by the children. Donald came out of the barn on a run. The dinner bell was also used as a summons in the time of trouble and this certainly was not dinnertime. Dag sat proudly behind the wheel and smiled broadly when he saw the gathering that had witnessed his first attempt at driving. The twins produced a towel for Dag to help wipe down the Packard and Bear said, "Anybody who drives has to help keep it clean."

Donald slowly approached and said, "I suppose now you will be badgering me to drive the truck. You know you will be competing with Joey for that." Joey was 14 years old now and had actually been driving the truck since he was 11. Dag looked at Joey and said, "Well, I reckon we can handle that, can't we, Joey?" Joey was grinning from ear to ear. The truth was that he had been after his grandfather to learn to drive more than once since he had been living with them.

When the household settled down for the night, Dag stuck his head into the bedroom where the twins slept and said, "I need to do a little thinkin' about sellin' the place but there ain't no problem with you buildin' yer little house down the road a bit. The corner where the roads cross might be a nice spot. Can't say but what I'd be glad to have you as a neighbor." They made a mutual decision to live in Dag's log cabin for the time being and wait until spring for a final decision.

Donald and Emily retired to their bedroom and prepared for bed. Donald was watching her with a gleam in his eye when he said, "I guess we can put Harlan to rest. Are you ready to marry me legal-like now, Em?" She gave him back a look with a gleam in her eye and answered, "You bet your booties, Granny!"

Chapter 27

CLAY - 1938

The old Buick limped down the road on its last breath of life. It had been making strange noises for the last 10 miles and Clay Harrington knew that it was about to die. He had already driven it 400 miles since he had stolen it in Nashville last Monday. Two little redheaded girls about 4 years old sat in the back seat, with big scared eyes. One of them was crying quietly and the other was trying not to. It wasn't that they were afraid of him. It was that they were hungry and they had come almost a hundred miles since morning on bumpy back roads. Even more than that, their mother had died a week ago. They weren't sure what 'died' meant but they thought it meant that she wouldn't be around any more. The old lady, Aunt Millie, the little family had lived with, had said she couldn't keep them. Somehow their daddy had got word about them and he had made an appearance at the door yesterday afternoon. They remembered him vaguely but never had known him well.

He could see a farmhouse on the left side of the road and it looked fairly prosperous. Maybe he could use the girls to wangle a meal out of the farmer. They did look kind of pitiful. It wasn't that he had no feeling for these two; he was between a rock and a hard place. He had been on the run for almost as long as they had been alive. He had participated in a bank robbery and just as sure as he was caught, he would spend the rest of his days in prison. Nancy had sent word to him that her days on earth were limited and she was worried about what would happen to the girls. Not only that, he had stolen this automobile and sooner or later that would catch up with him. He was headed for Michigan where his mother and Dad lived, for all the good that would do. They were both drunks and he doubted the girls would get much tender, loving care from either of them. The days of the Orphan Trains of 1850 to 1925 were over but there were now agencies to take care of unwanted children. He could not turn them over to anyone else without jeopardizing his own freedom Besides, he had enough feeling for these little girls to want to see them in a stable home. He knew his wife, Nancy, had loved them and done her best for them. He often wished that the times had been different and he could have managed to take care of his family himself.

The noise in the engine was getting louder and Clay swung into the driveway and was about to turn off onto the front lawn when intuition hit him and he kept right on going until he was around behind the barn when the engine died with a loud gasp and a backfire.

His entrance had not gone unnoticed. Emily was putting supper on the table when she looked out the kitchen window and saw an old car going on out to the barn. Curious as to what was going on, she called Donald to the window and said she thought she had seen some children in the back seat. He kept an old sock with a large bar of soap in it in a kitchen drawer to use as a weapon if the need arose. He took it out now and with it behind his back, approached the barn cautiously. Just as he was about to open the barn door, a man leading two little redheaded girls by the hand came from behind the corncrib. They were trying to hide behind him but Emily could see that it had been a while since they had seen soap and water. Seeing Donald's hand hidden behind him and not knowing what was in it, Clay quickly introduced himself. "Clay Dixon here," he said, skirting a little on his name as Donald might have seen some Wanted posters. "My daughters are named Molly and Ethel Grace. They are four years old and their mother died last week. We're on our way to Michigan to their grandparents."

"Why did you park around behind the barn?" Donald asked.

"I thought we might have to sleep in the car and I wanted it away from the road," Clay said, "and besides I need to look at the engine tomorrow. It's making a strange noise. We are mighty hungry and I have a little money. Could you possibly spare some food?" Donald relaxed and motioned for them to follow him. Once in the house Emily told Ruthie to take them into the washroom and clean them up for the table. Ruthie and Vernie were fascinated with the twins. Clay told his story while they were eating supper, leaving out his correct name and a few of the pertinent facts such as being wanted. Actually, in another day and time he might have been the respectable picture he painted of himself. After the meal, the girls and Vernie were nodding their heads and blinking their eyes to keep awake. Clay said, "If we could sleep in your barn, we'd be much obliged. Otherwise, we'll sleep in the car." Emily seemed to bristle at the idea of these two sweet little girls sleeping in the hay. "No, sir," she said, " the girls will be sleeping in a bed tonight. You can sleep in the barn." She went in to run a bath for them.

Clay went to the barn and found bedding in the harness room where Donald said it would be. Dag sort of hung around the kitchen as though something was on his mind. Finally he said, "Donald, somethin' ain't quite right about that fellow. I don't think we can trust him." Vern joined them in the kitchen then to put in his 2 cents worth. "I felt that, too, Dag, and I'd say it's none of our business as long as he behaves himself, but what about the two little girls? It can't be 'none of our business' as long as there's little ones that can't help themselves. They're not much older than Vernie." Donald came into the conversation, "They don't seem to be afraid of him, and they call him Daddy." "Well," Dag said, we'll see what tomorrow brings. He said he had to try to do somethin' to the car tomorrow. Maybe we'll get a chance to find out some about him."

When the blacksmith had come through a few months ago, Donald and Vern had approached him with a picture of a leather and metal arm shield with an iron hook on the end of it that they had found in a newspaper. The man had studied it and said, "I never saw anything like this before but it looks like it might work." Addressing Vern, he asked, "What did you do to your hand?" Vern told him briefly and stated that it had seemed to cut off his usefulness in this world. The smithy had studied him for a minute and said, "I think we can maybe fix that. It looks like a man could do a powerful lot of hoistin' and liftin' with a thing like this in place of a hand." He picked up one of his tools and started measuring Vern's arm every which way. "I'm gonna be out and around the countryside this week shoein' horses. I'll be in town on Saturday. Look me up and I'll tell you what I have decided." He tucked the piece of paper in his pocket and Donald distinctly felt the matter was closed.

When they went into town on Saturday, they found the man with his wagon and gear parked in behind the hardware store. He finished his business with a customer and went to his wagon where he pulled out something wrapped in newspaper. In it was what looked like an exact replica of the newspaper picture. He had worked on it at night in order to get it done by the end of the week. He had taken a liking to the man who wished to be useful again. Vern held up the stump of his arm and the smithy fitted the device on it and up over the elbow where there was a hinge so his elbow could bend naturally. Straps around the upper and lower arm held it firmly in place. There was about three quarters of an inch of extra space in the end where the hook was attached, and the smithy looked dismayed. But Vern said, " My stump is still pretty tender. Maybe Emmy can make something soft to go in there. When Donald asked how much they owed him, he said "Five dollars". Vern pulled his wallet out of his pocket and paid the man happily.

Clay and the girls had been at the farm about 2 weeks when the men made their move. The bonnet was up on the old car behind the barn and Clay was bent over the engine doing something with a wrench, thus, he didn't see them coming around the corner. Donald had a determined look on his face, Dag was squinting his eyes, and Vern had his left arm sticking out in front of him with the hook extended. Clay looked up and thought, "Oh! Oh! They know about me." Vern's hook intimidated him more than he liked to admit. The young man had the old sock in his hand again and Clay could see that there was something inside of it, probably some kind of a primitive weapon. One look at Dag's bearing and he figured the old man could do some damage whether he had a weapon or not. He straightened up and said, "What is it?" Dag spoke up, "We want to know what's going on. We don't think you been entirely honest with us. Those little girls ain't afraid of you, but they ain't very lovin' for bein' your daughters." Clay heaved a big sigh. They didn't know about him, but the open country faces made him want to ask them for help. "You're right," he said, "I need some help." Donald asked, "You ready to tell us a straight story?" As he finished speaking, Emily came around the corner of the barn, "Whatever it is you have to say, I want to hear it, too." She had a broom in her hand. Clay nodded his head, and said, "I guess since I'm gonna ask you for help, you all need to hear what I have to say. Let's sit on these benches outside the barn, here." They all got settled and he started in, "About the time my girls were born, we were pretty hard up. We needed money and I took part in a bank robbery over in Nashville, Tennessee." Dag burst forth with, "I knowed it! I knowed there was somethin' shady about you!" Clay went on, I couldn't go home because the Feds was after me, so I just sent money to Nancy whenever I could. That's why the girls are distant from me. I guess they just don't know me that well." He hesitated and Donald said, "We're not going to go against the law to help you." Clay came back with, "Not askin' you to. I can see that you people are good, honest people. I got a letter from Nancy saying that she had a bad sickness and there was nobody to take care of the twins. By the time I could get there she was in the last stages of dying from the cancer in her stomach. We're headed for Michigan where my folks live, but to tell you the truth, I'm not crazy about them taking care of my kids. They are drunks and they didn't do such a great job with me and my brother." Dag asked, "Where's your brother?" Clay continued, "He's an outlaw! I didn't know what else to do with them. Think what you want about me, but those little girls are innocent." "What do you want from us?" asked Vern. "I need to get out of here," Clay replied, "Will you keep Molly and Ethel Grace?" "Keep them? For how long?" Emily asked. "I don't know," replied Clay. "There's always a chance that the Feds will catch up with me." Donald said, "We will need to talk this over by ourselves this afternoon while the children are taking a nap. Will you take this old car with you? I don't think we want it around here."

After the children went down for their nap, the Morrisons went into the parlor for a discussion about the situation. It was decided that Emily would have two votes making 7 altogether, as she would have the brunt of taking care of them.

Vern took his turn first, "You know, we don't live very high on the hog ourselves. Can we afford to take on two more mouths to feed?"

Donald looked at Emily, "What if we have another baby? I know we don't plan to, but babies sometimes come along unbidden." He and Vern sometimes wondered how they had come to expand their household the way they had.

Ruthie clapped her hands and said, "Oh! They would be my little sisters, and they are so sweet"

Donald jumped in quickly, "Ruthie, you and Joey and all the rest of us would have to share what money we have for clothes, shoes, and food with them. Sometimes it's a tight squeeze now to buy a pair of shoes for somebody."

Dag was real thoughtful, "Would we be able to keep them for all time? I'd hate to get used to them and then have him come along one day and say he is ready to take them. Maybe we could make him sign a paper giving them to us."

Joey, who was now 15 years old, said, "I'd like 'em better if they was boys."

Emily was the only one who hadn't spoken. Now she said, "You are all wrong about one thing. They would not mainly be my responsibility. They would belong to all of us, including Joey who doesn't like girls. I don't have any idea if this Clay fellow is telling us the truth about anything. If he is an outlaw, how can we trust him? He could very well come back in a month, a year, or 2 years and say he wasn't serious and want them back. Maybe he stole them from their mother. There are a lot of negative things to be taken into consideration. Then we turn the page. When I was a little girl, the orphan trains used to come through town and people would look these boys and girls over like they were buying a horse, and some of them were. These kids wanted desperately for someone to want them and adopt them. You could see it in their eyes. I always thought how lucky I was that I had loving parents, not knowing at the time, my own history. I remember how they were 2 two weeks ago when they came here, hungry, scared, wanting their mama. Then I remember Joey and Ruthie sitting in the back seat with wide eyes, when our old car broke down. They were hungry, scared, wishing their daddy had come back for them. Only these two are standing off by themselves holding hands and wishing their mama was back. They don't even know their Daddy well enough to trust him to take care of them. I can't really believe that we need to vote but it's what we agreed on and we will carry it through." She passed a slip of paper to each participant and waited for the pencil to come around the circle. When everyone had placed their vote on the table, Donald went forward and picked them up.

There were 6 votes in favor of keeping the girls and one that said 'don't care'. Emily, with more than a little anger in her voice, said, " 'don't care' is not a passable vote. We will all go into the kitchen and come back in one at a time, and whoever voted 'don't care' will have a chance to say yea or nay." Joey, the errant voter, sensed that his mother was angry and couldn't see any advantage to voting nay so when they all came back into the parlor, all 7 votes said yea.

Donald looked directly at Joey and said, "Please go get Clay and tell him to come in, that we have decided." Joey wasn't exactly sulking. He well remembered the day the three of them had landed on the Morrison doorstep. He was just at an age where he felt duty bound to rebel against everything. He wasn't sulking, but his eyes were on the ground and therefore he was clear around behind the barn before he looked up. He stood there a few moments in stunned amazement when he realized there was no old Buick and no Clay anywhere in sight. He was galvanized into action when he thought he saw a slight movement back in the woods. Turning quickly, he ran toward the house yelling for Donald. Dag came running out of the door first saying, "Now! Now, Boy! What's all the ruckus about?" Donald, with the old sock in hand was next with Vern and his hook extended right behind them. The three of them looked like they were ready to fight Napoleon. And, of course, Emily followed with her broom.

"He's gone, and so is the car," Joey shouted. They all started for the barn at a fast pace as though they didn't believe the messenger and wanted to see for themselves. "Well," Vern said, "It looks like we had another voter who wanted to be shut of us."

Dag said, "It's probably for the best. At least he took the old car and didn't leave it for the Feds to find on our property. What do you want to bet it was stolen and he's goin' to dump it in Berryman's Stone Quarry? It's about 400 feet deep" There was a moment of silence and Vern said, "I think we would all do well to forget that last statement." The girls were coming out from the house and they were all distracted by a shriek from Ethel Grace. She had recognized a burlap bag back in the weeds as having been in the car with them and when they opened it, there was a ragged teddy bear (hers had been missing) and some clothes along with an envelope with Emily's name on it.

On inspection, there was a letter telling when the girl's birthday was (October 31, 1934), their names, and the fact that they had both had chicken pox in their short lives. This was written by their mother. Also in the envelope was a note from Clay that said, "I'm sorry to do this but I can't wait to hear your decision. If you can't take care of the girls, please see that they have a good home. I have serious doubts that you will ever see me again. I don't think anyone saw me here and Dixon is not the girl's real name but it will be better for you if you use it. Thanks for being such good people." Tucked into his note were ten $20 bills. "So," said Donald, he did have some money." Later, Vern took Donald aside and said, "That money may be marked. Best that you take it back by the tree stump in the cornfield and put it in the glass jar."

That night when Emily put the little ones to bed, Molly asked her, "Where did our Daddy go to? And why did he leave us?" Ethel Grace added, "Is he coming back to get us?" Emily had been thinking all afternoon what she was going to tell them, so she launched right into it. "Your Daddy had some problems to take care of and he couldn't do it with you girls along. He picked me and Donald to be your parents while he was gone. Vernie and Joey and Ruthie will be your brothers and sister and you will be sleeping in this bed every night from now on. You will have to learn how to do your share of the chores around here and I know you can't forget your mama but sometimes it works out well to have a spare mama waiting in the next room." She kissed them goodnight and tucked them in.

She and Vernie proceeded to his room where, with a worried look on his face, he asked, "Mama, would you and Daddy ever give me away?" "No, son," she said, but you will come to know that there are all different kinds of people in this world." Thoughtfully, he shut his eyes and drifted off to sleep.

Chapter 28

FLOYD DUNSMORE - 1939

Vern's new hand had indeed rendered him useful again. He was once more working in the fields and the barn with the other men. He could even milk the cows again using the Handy-Dandy milking machine that had come with the utilization of electricity on the farm. When he told Donald that it was the best $5 he ever spent, it made Donald proud for his part in procuring the artificial limb for his father. He hadn't tried driving the tractor but that was Joey's favorite job anyway and he doubted if he could be pried away from it. Donald was urging him to drive the truck and he thought he might enjoy driving again. He was working on the farm machinery that needed a second person to operate it. He had taken on the sole responsibility for operating the mechanics on the windmill that filled the large storage tank in the attic. The trick there was to fill it up without letting it run over and waste water. True, it had an overflow pipe that ran out of the side of the house, thus saving them from a horrible mess inside the house if someone forgot to turn off the windmill in time. It would be reflected upon in later years that adults who had weathered the Great Depression would never waste anything. They would forever 'clean up their plates', save their pennies, turn out the light when they leave the room, and eat the less desirable vegetables in the garden, sometimes even to the extent of serving cooked radishes for a meal. They would wear faded clothes with patches upon patches and half-sole their shoes when the holes in the bottom got too big. The rest of the story about the water tank was that when the tap was opened in the kitchen or washroom, gravity would carry the water to the bathtub, the kitchen sink, and the water closet for the commode.

Ruthie had also told Vern that she no longer had time to be the keeper of the swing board and she thought he could do it. This brought a smile to everyone's face as they remembered how he had assigned this chore to her when she and her brother and mother first came to the farm. Vernie and the girls were still using the beautiful carved swing board that said "Ruthie" on it that Donald had made for her first Christmas with the Morrisons. She was14 years old now and a great help to her mother. Emily quietly dreaded the next few years for Ruthie because she was getting to be a pretty girl and Emily could remember what that meant. It wasn't that she was displeased about Ruthie's looks. Maybe she was afraid of losing her too soon. Both she and Joey were going to high school in town. Perryville was a historic town and had been founded before the Revolution; therefore it was quite a progressive municipality. The high school was built in 1912, in time for Donald to attend it.

Joey was 16 years old and was 6'2", 4 inches taller than Donald. He played on the Viking's basketball team and was studying agriculture. Donald was very proud of him as Joey was more or less following in his footsteps.

Molly and Ethel Grace had been with them now for a year. At first they clung to each other and stayed by themselves. They had relaxed and now fit into the family nicely. Vernie had been largely responsible for the transition, and now the three were almost always together. The little ones all had their minor chores to do and Ruthie was planning to teach the girls to sew. They adored her, too, and had, in fact, started calling the other family members by family names. Emily felt a ghost passing overhead whenever she heard Mama, Daddy, Pop, and Grandpa. What if Clay would come back and tear them away? It would affect all of them, but it would devastate the girls. They would always think they weren't wanted. But she would rationalize that he was an outlaw and would not be back.

Vernie and the girls would start school next year together. There were 15 children of school age in the neighborhood now and the neighbors, in a joint effort had built a schoolhouse down on the corner a mile away. They had wanted Emily to teach but she felt she still had enough responsibilities at home to take care of without taking on more. She had taught her little ones the letters and numbers and each one of them knew how to print their names. She had always read stories to them so they already had a love of books.

Dag had proved to be worth his weight in gold. Even though he was on the slight side, his health was good and he managed to match Donald task for task. He had learned to drive the tractor and the truck. They had acquired 6 cows now and had a fairly healthy milk check every two weeks. He went back to Gulchy Gap a couple of times a year and stayed in his old house that the twins had left untouched when they bought his farm. They were now gentlemen farmers leasing out their fields to other farmers and keeping a couple of spirited horses in Old Prancer's barn to ride around to survey their holdings. They were now the special guests on Thanksgiving, Christmas, and any other time the mood struck them. They still drove the Packard 8 and wiped it off whenever they reached their destination. They let everybody, including Joey, drive it a bit when they came for a visit. Dag had settled in with the Morrisons and Emily doubted that even dynamite could budge him. Nobody seemed displeased that he was there and he certainly carried his own weight.

It was almost midnight on a Friday night in September when the household was awakened by a pounding on the back door. By the time Donald opened the door all three of the men were lined up behind him. Buck from the garage downtown was standing there. Doc had sent him out and he said, "When are you people goin' to get one of them telly-phones so Doc can quit getting me out of bed in the middle of the night to be his messenger?"

Vern, sensing that something important was going on, said "Never mind that, why are you here?"

Buck said "Oh! Yeah! Floyd has had a stroke and he is bad sick. Doc wants you and Donald to come right away."

Vern replied, even as he turned toward his bedroom to get dressed, "Tell him-"

"I ain't tellin' him nothin'. I'm goin' home to bed. You tell him," Buck shouted from his truck.

In half an hour Donald and Vern were letting themselves in the door at the Dunsmore residence. Doc came out of the bedroom to meet them, "Floyd had a massive stroke and I don't think he's going to make it. If he does, he'll be in sad shape."

"Where's Clara," Vern asked. Doc pointed toward the bedroom. "I'm glad you got here so quick. She needs to have somebody with her." When they entered the room, Clara looked up and said, "Oh, Vern, I'm so glad you're here, and you, too, Donald. I don't think he even knows I am here." As she said the last, she felt a slight squeeze on her hand that Floyd was holding. The three of them left the room and she told the men what she had felt. Vern said, "I think you're wrong about him not knowing. I think he could probably hear everything. I would like to talk to him alone. Is that all right with you, Clara?" She nodded her agreement and Vern went into the bedroom and shut the door.

He sat on the edge of the bed and Floyd hadn't stirred but Vern took his left hand in his. Doc had said the stroke had affected his right side, and he wanted to see if there would be any reaction when he said what he had to say. He cleared his throat and started, "Floyd, this is Vern. You probably know that already, but I have something I want to tell you. You gave me two of the most important things in my life. You gave me your daughter and my son. Now I'm going to give you something. You don't need to worry about Clara. I am going to come and live with her and take care of her for you. I'll help her with the store and I'll give her companionship." Vern waited a minute or two, and then said, "Did you hear me, Floyd? Did you understand me?" Ever so lightly, he felt a pressure on his hand. "This is a promise, Floyd, count on me to keep it." Half an hour later with Donald and Clara sitting next to his bed, he died quietly, at the age of 79.

They had been told by the undertaker, Simon Beck, to come in at 9:00 in the morning to make burial arrangements. Since they had left in such a hurry and brought no dress clothes, Donald decided to go home and come back in the morning. That way Emily would have a chance to pack some clothes for Vern to stay for a while. He had imparted his last conversation with Floyd to Donald, who just nodded his head slightly. He was very fond of his grandmother; he was torn between having his father move out of their home and being glad that there was somebody to take care of her.

The next morning Donald, Vern, and Clara arrived at the funeral home. Clara had a bag with some clothes to dress Floyd in and his best suit on a hanger. First of all, Clara said that she and Floyd had bought 6 plots in the cemetery when Flora died, looking at it being a family plot. Donald had not known this and was pleasantly surprised. She wanted to have a 1 o'clock funeral with the ladies of the Methodist church putting on a potluck dinner afterwards. Floyd was a longtime resident and businessman of Perryville and was well respected. She wanted all the 'bells and whistles' put into place for a man of his standing. She wanted the family to ride to the church and cemetery in the funeral car. There wasn't much for Vern and Donald to do except agree with her. She had it all planned in her mind.

When they arrived back at the house, she directed Vern to his new bedroom. She followed him in and said, "Vern, I want to thank you for coming to live here and be with me. I hope it is not too much of a hardship. I am 75 years old and don't feel that I could take care of all our affairs by myself. I guess you know that neither Floyd nor I took part in running the store much any more but that doesn't mean that you can't. Elmer Winters has been more or less managing it but he would like to sit back and rest a little more, and he never did come up with any ideas to make the store more modern. If we're going to hang on to it, that is exactly what we need to do."

Vern said, "Do you have any ideas, Clara? If you do maybe we can work together and spruce it up a little to make people want to come in. I have never been anything but a farmer, but I know how to manage money and maybe I can learn a few things about being a gentleman retailer."

Clara replied, "As a matter of fact, I do have some ideas. I have mostly seen you as a farmer but I know you are an honorable man, and I know you clean up pretty good. Everything we have will be Donald's some day and we need to take good care of it." Thus was sealed a good working agreement between Vern and Clara.

Chapter 29

THE RADIO

By the end of the week, Vern had moved all of his personal things that he wanted to take to live in the big house on Oakland Street. It was hard to tell if anyone was enthused by his move. They all put a good face on it because there was really no unselfish reason why he shouldn't do it. Donald had told him in private that he really hated to see him leave. He knew how much Vern had always loved the farm and it was still his. Vern had said many times that he was glad that Flora had been willing to live there as she had always been a city girl. Vern had replied, "Son, I raised you to be a good farmer and I trust you to do it well. Life changes, and when it does, we have to be willing to change with it. Would you and Emmy have wanted to bring your family to town to live and take care of your grandmother? Besides, she and I have been doing some planning and I think maybe I can get my life back on track better than I could on the farm. Donald was thoroughly mystified, but Vern did not offer to explain so he let it go.

Emily told him that they would be expecting him and Clara for Sunday dinner every week. She enjoyed having another woman in her life.

The family was sitting in the kitchen each pursuing their own amusement when Dag jumped to his feet and angrily said, "Dang it! What am I goin' to do for playin' checkies? I don't know why old Floyd had to go and die. If I should just go home maybe Bear or Garr would play with me."

Donald started laughing and said, "I can't see either one of them popinjay's playing checkers. They're too busy playing the rich landowners and riding their horses around their holdings- all 80 acres of it."

Ruthie giggled and Emily was smiling and before long Dag started laughing, too. Joey came into the kitchen carrying the checkerboard and said, "Teach me how to play, Grandpa, and I'll do it sometimes."

Dag, who had got a grip on his bad mood by then, said, "No, Joey, you don't need to do that. I was just bein' ugly 'cause I miss your Pop."

Joey thought a minute, and came back with, "I don't really want to play 'checkies', but I've got another idea. Did you ever play Solitaire?"

"You mean them little pieces of paper with the hearts on?"

"Yeah! One and the same."

"Never thought I'd care much for them games."

"Well, you won't know until you try." Joey left the room and came back with an old beat-up deck of cards. He laid them out on the table in Solitaire formation and began to explain to Dag the intricacies of playing with 'the little pieces of paper'. Dag began to ask questions and it wasn't long before he wanted to try it. By the end of the evening, he was a full-blown Solitaire fan.

When he came to breakfast the next morning, he was quiet and seemed to be a distance away. Emily hoped he wasn't truly thinking of going back home. She had grown to love the old man and wondered sometimes if she was trying to make up for all the years of separation. The meal was nearly finished when Dag spoke up, " I been thinkin'. Maybe we should get one of them there telly-phones. How do they work anyway?"

Joey, with a sly look on his face said, " They would put ours on the pole out by the road and give us a pair of shoes with cleats on so we could climb the pole and use it."

Dag said, "Oh, hush, boy. You know we never seen anybody climbin' those poles." Donald was looking down into his plate to hide the smile and Ruthie was giving Joey an interested look to see where this story was going. Joey was not finished and he said, "When you say hello into the telephone it goes like this: Hello Hello Hello Hello Hello **Hello Hello Hello Hello** until it gets where it's supposed to go and then it comes out of the wire like Hello."

Dag gave Joey a disgusted look, and said, "Now, boy, you don't need to think I just fell off the turnip truck yesterday. I ain't never talked on one of 'em but I got an idea it ain't like that."

Joey, loving to nettle his grandfather, said, " Swear to God it's true, Grandpa. I talked to the men when they were putting up the telephone poles and that's what they told me."

"Then they must still be laughing up their sleeves that they caught themselves a real rube."

Emily joined the conversation now, " I've had a few thoughts about a telephone. Do you remember how grumpy Buck was the night he came out to tell us about Grandfather? We're lucky that the line goes right past our house. Think how handy it would be if somebody got sick, like when Pop had his accident. What if one of the children would fall and break an arm while the autos were all away from the house? And Dad could call up his old friend, Vern when he got lonesome. We could even talk with Garr and Bear when we needed to. Joey and Ruthie could call us from school if they missed the school bus."

There was silence all around as they all thought of Emily's words and Donald reminded everybody that they would have to pay for each call they made. Then he conceded that maybe they did need one after all.

Joey and Donald had been to town for some bolts from the hardware store on an early June day. When they met back at the truck, Joey's face was lit up like a Christmas tree. When Donald asked him what was up, words came rushing out of his mouth like a freight train going through. " McKinnon's mint farm has posters up all over town." Donald said, yes, he had seen them.

"I want to work there this summer"

"It's the other side of town. How would you get there?"

"I would just have to get to town. They have a flatbed wagon to hook behind their pickup truck if they get too many to just ride in the truck. I figure as much traffic as there is on the highway now, it wouldn't be hard to get a ride if I hitch"

"Why this sudden push to work away from home? Don't I give you enough to do?"

"Sure, and I don't mind doing it, but there is something I want and I know I will have to earn the money for it. McKinnon pays $.50 an hour for hoeing weeds out of the mint fields."

"It's hot, dirty work, Joey, and you will have to quit when school starts. We're not going to let you off the hook on that."

"OK, but I need to call him back and let him know what I decided."

"Then you've already called him?"

"Sure, I needed to find out all the particulars."

"Well," Donald said, "We'll have to talk this over with the family and see what they say. Dag is almost 60 years old. Maybe he doesn't want to take on the work you would leave behind. And your mother certainly will have something to say about it."

Joey's face tensed up and Donald felt a pang for the boy he used to be. Of course, Joey was growing up. He undoubtedly had an eye for the girls. This wasn't the first time that Donald had felt a separation beginning. Hadn't his own father recognized his need for independence and even helped him with it? He said to Joey now, "Don't worry about it, son, I'll be on your side and do what I can to help you."

He needn't have fretted about it. That night when the family was gathered in the parlor, Joey told them about it, all except what he wanted the money for. He was adamant that it was going to be his secret. Dag said, "I know you been itchin' for a while boy, kind of like you got a burr under your saddle. I guess you're reachin' out to be a man, and there ain't nothin' wrong with that."

Donald said, "You've been a good worker and a lot of help, son. We'll miss you. Just make sure that if you're taking Mr. McKinnon's money you give him full value for it, no sloughing off when you get hot, tired, and dirty."

"Holy Moley, Donald, I'm not dying. Don't go missing me yet. And when did I ever slough off around here?"

Donald's sense of humor rose to the top and he gave a hearty laugh, which was the signal for Dag to give his funny little cackle.

Emily had been listening in silence and now rose from her chair and hugged Joey and kissed him tenderly on top of his head. Her little boy was indeed growing into a man.

It was the last week in August and school was about to start. According to the agreement, he gave Mr. McKinnon notice that Friday would be his last day. He was told that he would be welcomed back next summer, as he got out of the truck in town. He had to hurry and get to Montgomery Wards Catalog Store before it closed. He had been high on this moment all week.

The clerk recognized him immediately and said, "Say, Mister Jones, we have a package for you. It just came in this morning. Your mother was in but I didn't know if you would want me to tell her about it so I kept my 'tater trap' shut." He went into the backroom and came out with a box about 15x10x12. He looked at the billing papers on the box and said, "That'll be $9.53. Will that be cash?" Joey, looking a bit baffled, said, "Of course, what else would it be?" Embarrassed, the clerk said, "Lotsa folks using these new-fangled checks now," "Well," said Joey, "I'm not one of these new-fangled fellows." He paid for it and went out to the road where he would either catch a ride or walk the 5 miles home.

Happily, he had no more than put his thumb out when Harry Garza from over near Plum Blossom came along and stopped. Harry had picked him up several times that summer and liked the young man.

Emily and Ruthie were getting ready to put supper on the table. The twins were 5 years old now and one of their tasks was to set the table for every meal. Vernie thought that he had been let off the hook for housework until he found himself cleaning up the table every night.

Emily determined that she would fix a plate for Joey and put it in the warming oven as he was quite late getting home some nights. She had seen Donald and Dag out by the windmill cleaning themselves up for supper, but she stepped to the end of the porch anyway, to give the dinner bell a light tap. She heard a car coming down the road and thought maybe Joey would be in it. Sure enough, it stopped at the end of the driveway and Joey got out, but he had a box under his arm. Had she left something at the catalog store that morning? When he reached the porch, she still hadn't called out to him. "What have you got in the box, Joey?" she asked. He took it out from under his arm and looked at it like he had never seen it before. "I can't remember what it is, Mom. I'm thinking it's somebody else's. I'll take it back tomorrow. Or maybe it's that men's Eau De Cologne that I wanted to try." Emily knew that she wouldn't pull any more information out of him until he was ready to tell. He had been saying some strange things all week that she couldn't make any sense out of. He put the box in the washroom and they all sat down to supper. She could see that he was wrapped tight but it was in a happy sort of way. Everybody pitched in after supper, as they all knew that something was in the air.

When the last dishtowel was hung to dry, Joey went into the washroom and came out with the box. He set it on the table and was about to request a sharp knife when he looked down and Ethel Grace was standing there with a paring knife. He said, "Everybody has to make a guess as to what's in here." Here is what they guessed:

Dag- one of them telephones
Donald- title to a new car
Ruthie- a makeup kit for her and Mom
Vernie- a monkey (he had seen one in a book at school)
Molly- some new underwear with lace on it
Ethel Grace- some roller-skates
Emily- Men's Eau De Cologne

All of these suggestions were duly hashed over and scoffed at. Finally Joey slowly opened the box and, wonder of wonders, it was a small Philco table model radio. He explained that he was going to put it in the kitchen because Mom spent most of her time there. He also said in a sober voice that he had heard that there were some pretty startling things going on in Europe with a man named Adolph Hitler and he thought they had ought to keep abreast with the news.

He set the radio up on the kitchen table and produced an extension cord from his pocket and plugged it in. He took the instruction paper from the box and they all had a lesson in how to tune in the stations they wanted, set the volume, and unplugging it when not in use in case of a lightning storm. Donald was thinking of news, Emily was thinking of music, Dag was thinking of a program called 'Lum and Abner' that he had heard a little piece of at the hardware store. Joey had the baseball games in mind and Ruthie was thinking love songs and a boy at school named Gunter Drake. The littles were thinking about 'Jack Armstrong, the All-American Boy' sponsored by Wheaties cereal. The Martin boys at school had been telling them about it and they could hardly wait to hear it with their own ears.

Donald said that later when work slacked off on the farm, he would build a fancy shelf to put up in the kitchen for the 'Philco radio'. He didn't know it, but he had just coined a name for the new machine that would last for its lifetime. No one ever spoke of the radio without putting "Philco' before it. Donald stepped back and preened himself a bit, then said, "Now, I've got a surprise for all of you." They all sort of held their breath and waited to hear what it was. "When I was in town yesterday, I went into the telephone office and ordered a telephone put into the dining room." He waited a minute for this news to sink in, and said, "The crew will be here Monday morning to install it." There was another minute of stunned silence and Ruthie broke into a cheerleading call: " Donald! Donald! He's all right! He eats his Wheaties every night!" When the laughter and clapping had died down and not wanting to downplay Joey's gift, she broke into another: " Joey! Joey! What a sight! Hoes that mint with all his might!"

Chapter 30

SEE YOU AROUND, JOEY

Vern and Clara sat on the front porch of the big Victorian house on Oakland Street. It was twilight of an early spring day in 1941. Joey was 17 years old and about to graduate from Perryville High. The two adults were discussing what would be an appropriate gift for him. He had never had a formal suit and this was one of the gifts for sure. They wanted him to look like quality folk. Vern had brought in a good line of men's wear after he took over the store. Many of the men in church on Sunday were sprucing up the congregation with suits, shirts, and shoes from Dunsmore's Menswear. He had also dispensed with the groceries and hardware. He still maintained the yard goods department, because, while the economy was better, no one was yet out of the woods. The ladies' ready-to-wear was also still there but with a better quality of dresses. Molly had even enjoyed a pair of bloomers with lace around the legs. These were for Sunday, of course, when the whole family gussied up and attended the Methodist Church in town. Ethel Grace would have worn roller skates to church if she had any. There was a difference in personality between the twins like day and night. As it was, she had to settle for a matching pair of bloomers, much to her chagrin.

"Do you know what I've been thinking about, Vern?" Clara asked. When he acknowledged that he had no idea, she said, " A bridal store, that's what I've been thinking about."

"But, Clara," he said, "I haven't the first idea about what that would involve. Would we make it part of the regular store? Or would we have a separate building? If we put it in the building we have now, we would have to have larger fitting rooms, and even clerks that knew how to fit them to the women."

"I've thought of that," she said. "Ruthie will be out of school for the summer and she would probably like a job. Clarence Temple's oldest daughter has been studying design and I know that Clarence and Myrtle would be tickled to death for her to find something to keep her in Perryville."

"Do you think that would keep her here?"

"Myrtle thinks it would. She thinks Margaret is reluctant to make the break. I think she would be an asset in the store. She is quite a spiffy dresser and has a lot of couth. Myrtle says that she thinks Margaret could sell iceboxes to Eskimos." Vern gave a hearty laugh and Clara chuckled.

"Well, we're not going to sell iceboxes and we don't have any Eskimos in Perryville. Where does that leave us?"

"Back to the first square, do you think it might be worthwhile?"

Vern became serious again, " How much space would it take in the store and what would it cost to get an inventory set up?"

"We could clear out about 20 square feet of space back where we used to keep the brooms and household supplies. I think one fitting room for now would do, and granted, it would have to be a little larger to accommodate the wedding gowns. On second thought, maybe some pretty screens to set up around the fitting area would be better. Then we could move them to expand when we needed to. I sent for some bridal catalogs and thought we could start with them. If we order two nice wedding gowns and the accessories to display, I think we could do business out of the catalogs for a while. We would have to have someone well-versed in sewing, maybe Ruthie, to do alterations."

"It sounds like you've been doing your homework on this, Clara."

"Nobody ever sold a dirty pig, Vern. People will buy a clean one a lot quicker."

"It doesn't sound like a bad idea"

"And maybe you haven't noticed the number of young girls who are getting engaged. From the sound of the news in Europe we may be getting ready to have a war, and if that happens, a lot of young men will be going to fight, and a lot of girls will be wanting to get married."

Vern's demeanor turned very sober and he said, "Yes, young men like our Joey."

Clara said, "As much as I hate to admit it, this is true."

Vern said, "Well, I'm tired and I want to go to bed now. Why don't you get your catalogs around after supper tomorrow night and we will discuss it some more."

Emily and Donald were properly proud parents on graduation night as Joey went up to get his diploma. His new Dunsmore suit could hardly be seen for the gown he wore over it but his parents knew it was there. Ruthie, Vernie, Molly and Ethel Grace were there along with Dag, Vern, and Clara. Joey's girl friend, Claudia Green, was sitting 3 rows behind them. After the ceremony was over, they were all going to The Salt Box House for dinner. It was the fanciest eating place in town, not that the family ate out much, so this was a special treat for all of them. Ordinarily it would be supper but this was a special occasion so they called it dinner. Claudia was going with them and Joey came out of the gymnasium with his gown over his arm and his cap on askew. Ethel Grace watched Claudia and Joey covertly to see what they were doing. She knew that Joey liked Claudia a whole lot, but she wasn't too sold on the idea of Joey having a girl friend. He had always been a favorite of Ethel Grace and, even though she was only 6 years old, he belonged to her.

When asked if he had made up his mind what he would be doing now, he said that he figured on working for a year and saving his money to go to an agricultural school down in Georgia. His grandfather had already offered him a job at Dunsmore's Emporium. They all had a good time and when Joey left to take Claudia home, the rest of them left, also. The children belonged in bed at this time, but Donald and Emily were still in the kitchen when he came home. He acted like he had something to say so Donald said, "OK, what is it on your mind?" Joey hesitated, then supposed he might as well get it over: "You know things are heating up over in Europe." Donald and Emily both nodded. "Somebody is going to have to stop Hitler. England is trying and so is Russia. Even together they are not making a big splash with him. Everybody is speculating whether we are going to war or not." Emily could see where the conversation was going and gave a low moan. Joey held up his hand and continued, "If we go to war, I am going to enlist, and it probably wouldn't make any difference anyway, because the President said in his Fireside Chat on the Philco that congress is working on setting up a military draft, so I would probably have to go any way that you look at it." Then he bade them good night and went upstairs to bed. Emily and Donald sat in silence for about 10 minutes. With a deep sigh, Donald rose from his chair, took Emily's hand, and said, "If it happens, I guess we'll just have to bite the bullet, like a million other families. He's a man, Babe."

Joey went to work at Menswear with his grandfather and delved right in to learning as much as he could about business practices, accounting and public image. It was not what he wanted to do with his life, but he felt that life was sort of 'on hold' for the time being. The first Sunday in December, the whole family attended church, then hurried home because Vern and Clara would be coming out to dinner and there was yet another surprise when they reached home. The Packard 8 was sitting in the drive sparkling like a new penny. Dag, who was always glad to see his brothers, smiled broadly. Much to his surprise, when he opened the kitchen door, they were sitting at the table looking very sober, and the Philco was on. An announcer was talking excitedly about an attack of some kind. Joey and Donald stopped immediately and sat down at the table. Joey, in particular, had been following the news from around the world meticulously. He and Donald had discussed the state of the world at length. Soon the whole family including Vern and Clara were seated in some fashion in the kitchen, either in chairs brought in from other parts of the house or on the floor, but nobody was saying a word for fear that they might miss something being said on the Philco. The littles soon drifted off to other rooms as this did not hold their interest and they did not particularly like the mood in the kitchen.

The announcer continued with a history leading up to the attack.:

In October 1941 the naval general staff gave final approval to Yamamoto's plan, which called for the formation of an attack force commanded by Vice Admiral Chuichi Nagumo. It centered around six heavy aircraft carriers accompanied by 24 supporting vessels. A separate group of submarines was to sink any American warships, which escaped the Japanese carrier force. Nagumo's fleet assembled in the remote anchorage of Tankan Bay in the Kurile Islands and departed in strictest secrecy for Hawaii on 26 November 1941. The ships' route crossed the North Pacific and avoided normal shipping lanes. At dawn 7 December 1941, the Japanese task force had approached undetected to a point slightly more than 200 miles north of Oahu. At this time the U.S. carriers were not at Pearl Harbor. On 28 November, Admiral Kimmel sent USS Enterprise under Rear Admiral Willliam Halsey to deliver Marine Corps fighter planes to Wake Island. On 4 December Enterprise delivered the aircraft and on December 7 the task force was on its way back to Pearl Harbor. On 5 December, Admiral Kimmel sent the USS Lexington with a task force under Rear Admiral Newton to deliver 25 scout bombers to Midway Island. The last Pacific carrier, USS Saratoga, had left Pearl Harbor for upkeep and repairs on the West Coast.

At 6:00 a.m. on 7 December, the six Japanese carriers launched a first wave of 181 planes composed of torpedo bombers, dive bombers, horizontal bombers and fighters. Even as they winged south, some elements of U.S. forces on Oahu realized there was something different about this Sunday morning.

In the hours before dawn, U.S. Navy vessels spotted an unidentified submarine periscope near the entrance to Pearl Harbor. It was attacked and reported sunk by the destroyer USS Ward and a patrol plane. At 7:00 a.m., an alert operator of an Army radar station at Opana spotted the approaching first wave of the attack force. The officers to whom those reports were relayed did not consider them significant enough to take action. The report of the submarine sinking was handled routinely, and the radar sighting was passed off as an approaching group of American planes due to arrive that morning.

The Japanese aircrews achieved complete surprise when they hit American ships and military installations on Oahu shortly before 8:00 a.m. They attacked military airfields at the same time they hit the fleet anchored in Pearl Harbor. The Navy air bases at Ford Island and Kaneohe Bay, the Marine airfield at Ewa and the Army Air Corps fields at Bellows, Wheeler and Hickam were all bombed and strafed as other elements of the attacking force began their assaults on the ships moored in Pearl Harbor.

The purpose of the simultaneous attacks was to destroy the American planes before they could rise to intercept the Japanese.

Of the more than 90 ships at anchor in Pearl Harbor, the primary targets were the eight battleships anchored there. seven were moored on Battleship Row along the southeast shore of Ford Island while the USS Pennsylvania lay in drydock across the channel. Within the first minutes of the attack all the battleships adjacent to Ford Island had taken bomb and or torpedo hits. The USS West Virginia sank quickly. The USS Oklahoma turned turtle and sank. At about 8:10 a.m., the USS Arizona was mortally wounded by an armor piercing bomb which ignited the ship's forward ammunition magazine. The resulting explosion and fire killed 1,177 crewmen, the greatest loss of life on any ship that day and about half the total number of Americans killed. The USS California, USS Maryland, USS Tennessee and USS Nevada also suffered varying degrees of damage in the first half hour of the raid.

There was a short lull in the fury of the attack at about 8:30 a.m. At that time the USS Nevada, despite her wounds, managed to get underway and move down the channel toward the open sea. Before she could clear the harbor, a second wave of 170 Japanese planes, launched 30 minutes after the first, appeared over the harbor. They concentrated their attacks on the moving battleship, hoping to sink her in the channel and block the narrow entrance to Pearl Harbor. On orders from the harbor control tower, the USS Nevada (BB-36) beached herself at Hospital Point and the channel remained clear.

When the attack ended shortly before 10:00 a.m., less than two hours after it began, the American forces has paid a fearful price. Twenty-one ships of the U.S. Pacific Fleet were sunk or damaged: the battleships USS Arizona, USS California, USS Maryland, USS Nevada, USS Oklahoma, USS Pennsylvania, USS Tennessee and USS West Virginia; cruisers USS Helena, USS Honolulu and USS Raleigh; the destroyers USS Cassin, USS Downes, USS Helm and USS Shaw; seaplane tender USS Curtiss; target ship (ex-battleship) USS Utah; repair ship USS Vestal; minelayer USS Oglala ; tug USS Sotoyomo; and Floating Drydock Number 2. Aircraft losses were 188 destroyed and 159 damaged, the majority hit before they had a chance to take off. American dead numbered 2,403. That figure included 68 civilians, most of them killed by improperly fused anti-aircraft shells landing in Honolulu. There were 1,178 military and civilian wounded.

Japanese losses were comparatively light. Twenty-nine planes, less than 10 percent of the attacking force, failed to return to their carriers. The Japanese success was overwhelming, but it was not complete. They failed to damage any American aircraft carriers, which by a stroke of luck, had been absent from the harbor. They neglected to damage the shoreside facilities at the Pearl Harbor Naval Base. American technological skill raised and repaired all but three of the ships sunk or damaged at Pearl Harbor (the USS Arizona considered too badly damaged to be salvaged, the USS Oklahoma raised and considered too old to be worth repairing, and the obsolete USS Utah considered not worth the effort). Most importantly, the shock and anger caused by the surprise attack on Pearl Harbor united a divided nation and was translated into a wholehearted commitment to victory in World War II.

The women finally made coffee and sandwiches for the assembled group but the atmosphere remained charged with sobriety and the Philco remained tuned in to the happenings of the day lest they miss something important.

The next day, December 8, 1941, President Roosevelt, famous for his Fireside Chats, was on the Philco with his famous 'Day of Infamy speech and again, the residents of the Morrison household didn't miss a word:

Fireside Chat 19 (December 9, 1941)

On the War with Japan

My fellow Americans:

The sudden criminal attacks perpetrated by the Japanese in the Pacific provide the climax of a decade of international immorality.

Powerful and resourceful gangsters have banded together to make war upon the whole human race. Their challenge has now been flung at the United States of America. The Japanese have treacherously violated the longstanding peace between us. Many American soldiers and sailors have been killed by enemy action. American ships have been sunk; American airplanes have been destroyed.

The Congress and the people of the United States have accepted that challenge.

Together with other free peoples, we are now fighting to maintain our right to live among our world neighbors in freedom, in common decency, without fear of assault.

I have prepared the full record of our past relations with Japan, and it will be submitted to the Congress. It begins with the visit of Commodore Parry to Japan eighty-eight years ago. It ends with the visit of two Japanese emissaries to the Secretary of State last Sunday, an hour after Japanese forces had loosed their bombs and machine guns against our flag, our forces and our citizens.

I can say with utmost confidence that no Americans today or a thousand years hence, need feel anything but pride in our patience and in our efforts through all the years toward achieving a peace in the Pacific which would be fair and honorable to every nation, large or small. And no honest person, today or a thousand years hence, will be able to suppress a sense of indignation and horror at the treachery committed by the military dictators of Japan, under the very shadow of the flag of peace borne by their special envoys in our midst.

The course that Japan has followed for the past ten years in Asia has paralleled the course of Hitler and Mussolini in Europe and in Africa. Today, it has become far more than a parallel. It is actual collaboration so well calculated that all the continents of the world, and all the oceans, are now considered by the Axis strategists as one gigantic battlefield.

In 1931, ten years ago, Japan invaded Manchukuo — without warning. In 1935, Italy invaded Ethiopia — without warning. In 1938, Hitler occupied Austria — without warning.

In 1939, Hitler invaded Czechoslovakia — without warning. Later in '39, Hitler invaded Poland — without warning.

In 1940, Hitler invaded Norway, Denmark, the Netherlands, Belgium and Luxembourg — without warning.

In 1940, Italy attacked France and later Greece — without warning. And this year, in 1941, the Axis Powers attacked Yugoslavia and Greece and they dominated the Balkans — without warning.

In 1941, also, Hitler invaded Russia — without warning. And now Japan has attacked Malaya and Thailand — and the United States — without warning.

It is all of one pattern.

We are now in this war. We are all in it — all the way. Every single man, woman and child is a partner in the most tremendous undertaking of our American history. We must share together the bad news and the good news, the defeats and the victories — the changing fortunes of war.

So far, the news has been all bad. We have suffered a serious setback in Hawaii. Our forces in the Philippines, which include the brave people of that Commonwealth, are taking punishment, but are defending themselves vigorously. The reports from Guam and Wake and Midway Islands are still confused, but we must be prepared for the announcement that all these three outposts have been seized.

The casualty lists of these first few days will undoubtedly be large. I deeply feel the anxiety of all of the families of the men in our armed forces and the relatives of people in cities which have been bombed. I can only give them my solemn promise that they will get news just as quickly as possible. This Government will put its trust in the stamina of the American people, and will give the facts to the public just as soon as two conditions have been fulfilled: first, that the information has been definitely and officially confirmed; and, second, that the release of the information at the time it is received will not prove valuable to the enemy directly or indirectly.

Most earnestly I urge my countrymen to reject all rumors. These ugly little hints of complete disaster fly thick and fast in wartime. They have to be examined and appraised.

As an example, I can tell you frankly that until further surveys are made, I have not sufficient information to state the exact damage which has been done to our naval vessels at Pearl Harbor. Admittedly the damage is serious. But no one can say how serious, until we know how much of this damage can be repaired and how quickly the necessary repairs can be made.

I cite as another example a statement made on Sunday night that a Japanese carrier had been located and sunk off the Canal Zone. And when you hear statements that are attributed to what they call "an authoritative source," you can be reasonably sure from now on that under these war circumstances the "authoritative source" is not any person in authority.

Many rumors and reports which we now hear originate, of course, with enemy sources. For instance, today the Japanese are claiming that as a result of their one action against Hawaii they have gained naval supremacy in the Pacific. This is an old trick of propaganda which has been used innumerable times by the Nazis. The purposes of such fantastic claims are, of course, to spread fear and confusion among us, and to goad us into revealing military information which our enemies are desperately anxious to obtain.

Our Government will not be caught in this obvious trap — and neither will the people of the United States.

It must be remembered by each and every one of us that our free and rapid communication these days must be greatly restricted in wartime. It is not possible to receive full and speedy and accurate reports from distant areas of combat. This is particularly true where naval operations are concerned. For in these days of the marvels of the radio it is often impossible for the Commanders of various units to report their activities by radio at all, for the very simple reason that this information would become available to the enemy and would disclose their position and their plan of defense or attack.

Of necessity there will be delays in officially confirming or denying reports of operations, but we will not hide facts from the country if we know the facts and if the enemy will not be aided by their disclosure.

To all newspapers and radio stations — all those who reach the eyes and ears of the American people — I say this: You have a most grave responsibility to the nation now and for the duration of this war.

If you feel that your Government is not disclosing enough of the truth, you have every right to say so. But in the absence of all the facts, as revealed by official sources, you have no right in the ethics of patriotism to deal out unconfirmed reports in such a way as to make people believe that they are gospel truth.

Every citizen, in every walk of life, shares this same responsibility. The lives of our soldiers and sailors — the whole future of this nation — depend upon the manner in which each and every one of us fulfills his obligation to our country.

Now a word about the recent past and the future. A year and a half has elapsed since the fall of France, when the whole world first realized the mechanized might which the Axis nations had been building up for so many years. America has used that year and a half to great advantage. Knowing that the attack might reach us in all too short a time, we immediately began greatly to increase our industrial strength and our capacity to meet the demands of modern warfare.

Precious months were gained by sending vast quantities of our war material to the nations of the world still able to resist Axis aggression. Our policy rested on the fundamental truth that the defense of any country resisting Hitler or Japan was in the long run the defense of our own country. That policy has been justified. It has given us time, invaluable time, to build our American assembly lines of production.

Assembly lines are now in operation. Others are being rushed to completion. A steady stream of tanks and planes, of guns and ships and shells and equipment — that is what these eighteen months have given us. But it is all only a beginning of what still has to be done. We must be set to face a long war against crafty and powerful bandits. The attack at Pearl Harbor can be repeated at any one of many points, points in both oceans and along both our coast lines and against all the rest of the Hemisphere. It will not only be a long war, it will be a hard war. That is the basis on which we now lay all our plans. That is the yardstick by which we measure what we shall need and demand; money, materials, doubled and quadrupled production — ever-increasing. The production must be not only for our own Army and Navy and air forces. It must reinforce the other armies and navies and air forces fighting the Nazis and the war lords of Japan throughout the Americas and throughout the world.

I have been working today on the subject of production. Your Government has decided on two broad policies.

The first is to speed up all existing production by working on a seven day week basis in every war industry, including the production of essential raw materials.

The second policy, now being put into form, is to rush additions to the capacity of production by building more new plants, by adding to old plants, and by using the many smaller plants for war needs.

Over the hard road of the past months, we have at times met obstacles and difficulties, divisions and disputes, indifference and callousness. That is now all past — and, I am sure, forgotten.

The fact is that the country now has an organization in Washington built around men and women who are recognized experts in their own fields. I think the country knows that the people who are actually responsible in each and every one of these many fields are pulling together with a teamwork that has never before been excelled.

On the road ahead there lies hard work — grueling work — day and night, every hour and every minute.

I was about to add that ahead there lies sacrifice for all of us. But it is not correct to use that word. The United States does not consider it a sacrifice to do all one can, to give one's best to our nation, when the nation is fighting for its existence and its future life. It is not a sacrifice for any man, old or young, to be in the Army or the Navy of the United States. Rather it is a privilege. It is not a sacrifice for the industrialist or the wage earner, the farmer or the shopkeeper, the trainmen or the doctor, to pay more taxes, to buy more bonds, to forego extra profits, to work longer or harder at the task for which he is best fitted. Rather it is a privilege. It is not a sacrifice to do without many things to which we are accustomed if the national defense calls for doing without it.

A review this morning leads me to the conclusion that at present we shall not have to curtail the normal use of articles of food. There is enough food today for all of us and enough left over to send to those who are fighting on the same side with us.

But there will be a clear and definite shortage of metals for many kinds of civilian use, for the very good reason that in our increased program we shall need for war purposes more than half of that portion of the principal metals which during the past year have gone into articles for civilian use. Yes, we shall have to give up many things entirely.

And I am sure that the people in every part of the nation are prepared in their individual living to win this war. I am sure that they will cheerfully help to pay a large part of its financial cost while it goes on. I am sure they will cheerfully give up those material things that they are asked to give up. And I am sure that they will retain all those great spiritual things without which we cannot win through.

I repeat that the United States can accept no result save victory, final and complete. Not only must the shame of Japanese treachery be wiped out, but the sources of international brutality, wherever they exist, must be absolutely and finally broken.

In my Message to the Congress yesterday I said that we "will make very certain that this form of treachery shall never endanger us again." In order to achieve that certainty, we must begin the great task that is before us by abandoning once and for all the illusion that we can ever again isolate ourselves from the rest of humanity.

In these past few years — and, most violently, in the past three days — we have learned a terrible lesson.

It is our obligation to our dead — it is our sacred obligation to their children and to our children — that we must never forget what we have learned.

And what we have learned is this:

There is no such thing as security for any nation — or any individual — in a world ruled by the principles of gangsterism. There is no such thing as impregnable defense against powerful aggressors who sneak up in the dark and strike without warning. We have learned that our ocean-girt hemisphere is not immune from severe attack — that we cannot measure our safety in terms of miles on any map any more.

We may acknowledge that our enemies have performed a brilliant feat of deception, perfectly timed and executed with great skill. It was a thoroughly dishonorable deed, but we must face the fact that modern warfare as conducted in the Nazi manner is a dirty business. We don't like it — we didn't want to get in it — but we are in it and we're going to fight it with everything we've got.

I do not think any American has any doubt of our ability to administer proper punishment to the perpetrators of these crimes.

Your Government knows that for weeks Germany has been telling Japan that if Japan did not attack the United States, Japan would not share in dividing the spoils with Germany when peace came. She was promised by Germany that if she came in she would receive the complete and perpetual control of the whole of the Pacific area — and that means not only the Ear East, but also all of the Islands in the Pacific, and also a stranglehold on the west coast of North, Central and South America.

We know also that Germany and Japan are conducting their military and naval operations in accordance with a joint plan. That plan considers all peoples and nations which are not helping the Axis powers as common enemies of each and every one of the Axis powers.

That is their simple and obvious grand strategy. And that is why the American people must realize that it can be matched only with similar grand strategy. We must realize for example that Japanese successes against the United States in the Pacific are helpful to German operations in Libya; that any German success against the Caucasus is inevitably an assistance to Japan in her operations against the Dutch East Indies; that a German attack against Algiers or Morocco opens the way to a German attack against South America and the Canal.

On the other side of the picture, we must learn also to know that guerilla warfare against the Germans in, let us say Serbia or Norway, helps us; that a successful Russian offensive against the Germans helps us; and that British successes on land or sea in any part of the world strengthen our hands.

Remember always that Germany and Italy, regardless of any formal declaration of war, consider themselves at war with the United States at this moment just as much as they consider themselves at war with Britain or Russia. And Germany puts all the other Republics of the Americas into the same category of enemies. The people of our sister Republics of this Hemisphere can be honored by that fact.

The true goal we seek is far above and beyond the ugly field of battle. When we resort to force, as now we must, we are determined that this force shall be directed toward ultimate good as well as against immediate evil. We Americans are not destroyers — we are builders.

We are now in the midst of a war, not for conquest, not for vengeance, but for a world in which this nation, and all that this nation represents, will be safe for our children. We expect to eliminate the danger from Japan, but it would serve us ill if we accomplished that and found that the rest of the world was dominated by Hitler and Mussolini.

So we are going to win the war and we are going to win the peace that follows. And in the difficult hours of this day — through dark days that may be yet to come — we will know that the vast majority of the members of the human race are on our side. Many of them are fighting with us. All of them are praying for us. But, in representing our cause, we represent theirs as well — our hope and their hope for liberty under God.

Joey, who had gone to work as usual, came home all excited. As young men had been, down through the ages, he was excited about going to war. Vern had acquired a small radio from somewhere and set it up in the menswear department. It had been on all day and Joey now said, "Sheriff Roy was in the store today and he says there will be a recruiting office set up in town in less than a week. As soon as they start to take enlistments, I am going to enlist." Emily struggled to know what to say to her son who had been a baby just yesterday, or so it seemed. Finally she nodded her head, ever so slightly, in Donald's manner, and said, "Of course, son, I would expect nothing less."

Chapter 31

THE SOLDIER

In one week the recruiting office had been established and was ready for business. On Monday, December 15, 1941, when Lieutenant Frith opened the door at 9 o'clock, there was a line of Perryville's young men stretching down the street for six blocks. Where in the world did they all come from? he asked himself. The War Department had given him one assistant so his first order of business was to call the number in Washington and tell them he needed two more people temporarily. He could all but hear them laughing when they told him that maybe he could pick a couple of likely looking young fellows out of the crowd to help. He knew what that meant. It meant that the pay for these people would come out of his pocket. The second order of business, it seemed would be to organize a system. Lieutenant Frith was a very efficient man. He had boxes of enlistment forms in the back room, but they were no good without manpower. He and his helper, Sergeant Bloomfield, went outside and locked the door. Groans came from the crowd of young men. He started talking loudly, "We've got a situation here that we've never dealt with before. We had no idea that there would be so many of you, so first we want to thank you for coming forth to defend your country. You will have to be patient while we get ready." Then, realizing that only a few right at the front could hear what he said, he turned to the first 6 boys in line, "Go back down the line and stop about every 30 feet and tell them there has been a delay. The last three blocks tell them to go home and check this afternoon to see how things are. The war will still be on tomorrow. Report back here to me." He motioned to Bloomfield and they turned around and went back inside. "How good are you at typing, Bloomfield?" The sergeant shrugged his shoulders and said, "Fair, I guess." "All right, type me up a document as quick as you can stating that we will handle 10 men at a time inside the office, a line one block long is all we can process at a time. The rest can go home and be back here at one o'clock to see how things are going. Run me off 50 copies on the mimeograph machine and I will start distributing them. When I am almost out, I will send somebody back after more. Oh, and be sure to tell them we appreciate their patriotism." In 15 minutes he started down the line handing out copies every 6 feet or so, while the sergeant stayed in the office and made copies. He was also looking the crowd over for someone he figured could really help him. When he got to the end of the line he turned and started back. He was looking for a tall boy he'd seen that seemed to command his mates' respect. He had noticed several of them and by the time he got back he had beckoned four of them to follow him, one of which was Joey. Inside, he turned to them and said, " I need some help here desperately for the next couple of days. I don't have any money to pay you for your services, but I will give you a letter of commendation, for what it's worth, if you will help me process this first onslaught. This other man is Sergeant Bloomfield and we should be able to take care of things later. I am really impressed that there are so many young men who want to defend their country." There were four folding tables in the back room and the boys soon had them set up and supplies on each one. After a 10 minute 'crash course in what they were to do, Frith went to the door. That was when he realized he needed traffic control; otherwise, they would all come piling in at once. He picked two sturdy-looking fellows from the first group and took them inside explaining that they were to allow 15 men into the office then replacing each one that left with a new one. There were 10 school chairs against one wall with big arms so they could fill out their papers. When the office closed at 5 o'clock, many of them had become cold and tired and had gone home. Joey asked the sergeant when the workers were going to get to enlist. He chuckled, and said, " Afraid it will be over before you get there?" Then he added, "Come in at 7:30 in the morning and you can do it then, but we would still like to have you help us some more. It will probably take a week for things to calm down to where the sergeant and I can handle it."

That night at the supper table Joey recounted the day's events and told how the lieutenant was going to give him a letter of commendation. Dag snickered and said, "Who you goin' to show this letter to, boy? The Japs?" Donald looked at Joey's deflated face and said, "That's enough, Dag, he's going to show it to us and his mama is going to keep it for him until he gets home. He is proud of himself for stepping in to help in a bad situation, and rightly so!" Dag seemed to be examining something on his plate that was very intriguing. Then he looked straight at Joey, and said, "I'm sorry, Joey that was a mean thing to say. Donald is right. Always be proud to be useful and willing to do whatever there is to do." Joey smiled and said, "That's the way I feel about it, Grandpa, and I am proud that he picked me out of 600 people standing there. He must have seen something in me that was special." Dag rose from his chair and went around the table, put his arms around Joey's neck and said, "Danged right he did, 'cause there's a lot of special inside your long, lanky hide." After Joey went to his bedroom, there was a timid knock on the door. Ruthie was standing there with an apprehensive look. Joey bade her come in and said, "There is something I want to talk to you about." As though she wanted to get the first word in, she burst out: "Joey, we've been pretty close and I know you don't want any of us worrying about you, but we are going to. We can't help it. We're also going to be very proud of you," and she threw her arms around his neck. She managed to keep the tears at bay, because she knew they had to send him off on a cheerful note. Then he said, "There is something I'm going to ask of you, though. I want to marry Claudia before I am shipped overseas. We got carried away Saturday night last week and if she should find herself carrying a baby she would need a friend. Can I tell her that you will be that friend?" Momentarily stunned, she finally said, " Yes, you mean to stand with her against anyone who might give her grief?" Joey said, "Yes, I don't think Mom and Donald would but her folks might. I don't really think it is going to happen the first time, but I don't know." She nodded her head slowly, "That's a promise, brother."

Joey and the other helpers signed up the next morning before the doors were opened, and the Lieutenant was wrong. The janitor from the high school arrived at 8 o'clock with a load of 10 student's chairs for the office to use until the crisis was over. This meant they could process twice as many enlistments. It only took 3 days for things to slow down enough so that Joey and his friends could quit helping. The Sergeant had put a notice on the bulletin board that three buses would be at the office to pick up the first 135 enlistees to start them on their way to boot camp on Friday morning, January 5, 1942 at 8 o' clock. It said, "Don't bring anything but the clothes on your back." The schedule would be:

Friday- 1 through 135
Saturday- 136 through 270
Sunday- 271 through 405
Monday- 406 through 540
All numbers after 540 will be notified when their bus will leave. There will be a penalty for failing to arrive at boot camp when expected. The name of the boot camp and the branch of the service would be determined as the men boarded the buses.

Since Joey's number was 329, he would be expected to leave with Sunday's group. He figured he needed to spend most of his time saying good-bye to his friends and family. He also needed to tie up some loose ends of his finances and see Claudia as much as possible.

The next morning Joey was out and about at the barn and he began to catch sight of movement out of the corner of his eye. Knowing it was Vernie and the girls, he tried to ignore it, but when he came around the corner of the barn and literally fell over Molly, he said, "What's going on? What are you kids following me around for? Why are you spying on me?"

"Why are you goin' away, Joey," Vernie asked him. "Who's going to teach me to ride a bicycle when I get one?" Vernie had seen a 2-wheeled bike at the hardware store and it had occupied his thoughts a good portion of his waking hours.

"Are you and Claudia going to get married? I heard Mr. Dobbins at Pop's store say you probably would. Now that all the boys are going into the service, they're all going to be hot to trot to get married," Molly contributed.

Joey looked at Ethel Grace to see what she would have to offer, as he knew it would be something to require a careful answer. She opened her mouth but no words came out, which was strange in itself. He could see that tears were beginning to flow, and she said, "But, Joey, who's going to tell me not to get mad when somebody teases me? You know, Mama says I have a hard time controlling my temper. And besides, I love you and I want to marry you some day. Old Claudia can find somebody else"

Joey quickly realized that these were serious problems as all three were in tears now. "Let's take Vernie's concern first. You know about the war, Vernie. You know that is why I have to go. The Japs bombed Pearl Harbor and killed a lot of our men, and they haven't quit. As far as the bicycle is concerned, who do you think taught me to ride one? Your Daddy did. He ran up and down the driveway hanging on to the seat to help me find my balance until I found it. Mama did sometimes, too, and both Grandpas did some but maybe they are too old to do that now. They helped Ruthie, too. You be a good boy and help as much as you can because I'm not going to be here to do my share of the work, so you need to step in and take up some of the slack. Will you promise me you'll do that? And take care of Mama, all of you because she is going to feel bad that I am gone." Vernie brightened up and nodded his head.

Now he looked at the girls and put out his arms, motioning them to come to him. He said, "I don't know yet about marrying Claudia, Molly. I think I love her but I've never been in love before so I'm not sure. If I did, she would be part of our family and she would be your sister-in-law, and I would want you to treat her with respect, like you do with Ruthie." Molly asked, "Would she live with us?" Joey responded, "I haven't even asked her yet, and I don't want you kids saying anything to her about it. Will you promise me?" Molly and Vernie agreed, but Joey could see that the hardest part of the trio was ahead of him.

"Ethel Grace, I sure am proud that you love me and think I would make you a good husband, but it would be impossible. Don't you see? Brothers and sisters can't get a license to get married and you are my sister." Her face clearly showed that this was a revelation. I don't like to hear you say, 'Old Claudia', either. It is disrespectful and she is going to need all of you to be her friends." Finally, the little girl seemed reconciled to the inevitable, and Joey said, "Now, go play and quit following me around." He could almost believe that he had dodged a bullet.

Later in the day, Donald asked him to help him replace a fence post down the lane. He seemed to have something on his mind. By now Joey had caught on that they all had something on their minds. They went on about the business of fixing the fence post when Donald said, "You going to think of me once in a while when you're gone?"

Joey put one foot up on the fence and said, "You know, Donald, I've been storing up memories for everybody. Things that have pleased me and made us all laugh."

Donald queried, "What have you got stored up for me?"

"Do you remember the time when I was about 11 and had just learned to drive the truck, and you and I went back to the woods to get a load of firewood?"

"Yeah, it was in October, if I remember right, and it had been raining all week. I don't know what I was thinking."

"We got that old pickup all loaded and were ready to get in it and take off when we noticed that the back wheels had sunk clear to the axle. I remember we just stood there looking at each other for what seemed like forever."

"I remember, Joey, first I got in and tried to drive while you pushed."

Joey broke into gales of laughter, "As if a skinny little 11 year old kid could make a difference in whether we got unstuck or not. But then you got out and told me to drive, and you'd push. You didn't make much difference, either. I started laughing and I thought you were going to get mad but then we were both laughing. Or crying, I was never sure which."

"When we finally decided that we had to unload the wood, it wasn't funny any more. That wood left the pickup easier than it went in, except that we were almost worn out by then."

"Then we found out that we were just not going to do it by ourselves and would have to get the tractor; you wanted me to stay there and wait, but I was dang near freezin'. By the time we got to the house, Mom was near ready to send out the troops to find us."

"Yeah," Donald said, "I was sure glad that she set her foot down and made us wait until morning to go back to the woods."

"And besides Pop went with us and I was sure glad we had another pair of hands. I wasn't havin' any real big love affair with all that wood by then." They had finished setting the fence post and climbed into the truck and started for the house.

Just before suppertime Saturday night, Bear and Garr rolled up the drive in the Packard 8. Dag had said he thought they were coming to see Joey off and Emily had had an eye on the road all day for them. After they wiped all the dust off the car, they opened the boot and took out a suitcase and a clothing bag that snapped up the front. Ethel Grace ran out to meet them, with Molly a little bit behind her. "What's in there?" she asked and pointed at the bag. Bear said, "Why, honeybunch, that's our good clothes. Aren't you going to dress up in your good clothes to say good-bye to Joey?" Clearly, she hadn't given it too much thought, however, she said, "Sure, we're going to wear our Sunday dresses and I'm going to ask Mama if we can carry our Sunday School pocketbooks." Garr spoke up then and said, "The native Indians used to stare at something intensely that they wanted to remember and claimed they were taking a picture and storing it in their heads. May be that is what Joey will do and we want him to have a nice picture, don't we?"

Clara and Vern were there and after supper, Vern wanted Joey to go to the orchard with him. A bit puzzled, Joey slipped his jacket on and was almost to the barn before he noticed that it was a full moon. Then it came to him what Vern was doing. He was telling Joey good-bye in his own fashion. Vern said,

"You remember how I used to show you the constellations and the different stars, son?" "Sure," Joey said, "How could I forget?" and he pointed to the North Star. "Well," Vern said, wherever you go, you will be looking at the same sky as we are right now. I don't know, maybe things will be positioned in a little different place than they are from here. But wherever you look, know that the ones that love you will be standing under the same stars." He turned toward Joey and put his arms out and Joey stepped into them. "I'll remember that, Pop!" he said.

Chapter 32

DETROIT CITY

Emily was up and had breakfast on the table at 5:30 the next morning, There was a little grumbling as the family began to wake up, somewhat unwillingly, but it soon came to a halt when Emily reminded them that Joey was leaving and he would not leave her house without a good breakfast inside him. It didn't take long for a lively conversation to ensue along with hearty laughter and giggles from the 'littles'. Emily had a schedule for the bathroom and soon everyone was putting on their Sunday clothes as they were going to church after the bus left, anyway. Bear and Garr had a new-fangled electric shaver so they didn't need the washroom too long. Everybody had bathed the night before, so by 7 o'clock, everybody but the Brown twins had assembled for Emily and Ruthie to apply the finishing touches. The bedroom door upstairs opened and all eyes flew to the top of the stairs. There stood Bear and Garr in all their splendor in identical tuxedoes, black shoes and socks, and spats. In the moment of silence, a little piece of Joey died a thousand deaths, but quickly came back to life when he saw Grandpa Dag looking at him. He was more than a little ashamed of himself when he thought about the effort they had put forth for him, and he knew it was for him, and he would have to say the right thing. He opened his mouth and pronounced, "Uncle Bear! Uncle Garr! You look like princes coming to the coronation. If this is for me, I thank you." It must have sufficed for they both broke into broad grins and started out the door, with the rest of the company following.

There were 135 men leaving for boot camp and about 200 family members milling around. Emily noted that some of the boys didn't seem to have any family there, and she thought that was terrible. Then Donald reminded her that some of these boys were from as far away as Blossom Falls, which was a good 100 miles away, and undoubtedly, had said their good-byes closer to home. He knew that some of these hill families still had only mules and wagon to travel in. In fact, probably some of these boys had spent 3 days walking and hitching rides to get here. He had heard that some of them had been sleeping in the woods east of town since the first enlistment day. The townspeople had even set up an Enlistment Kitchen in the First Methodist Church Basement to feed them. It was probably the pre-cursor to the USO, which voluntarily fed and slept traveling military troops throughout the war.

At 8 o'clock, the families were asked to leave and the task of assigning the men to different branches of the military and getting them on buses began. Joey was assigned to the US Army and was one of the first ones on the bus. As he had his choice of seats he picked one in the middle by the window. Right behind him was a rather strange boy from up in the hills that he knew vaguely from helping in the recruiting office. His name was Blooper Adams and when he appeared to want to sit down, Joey almost objected. But being well raised by his mama, he motioned for him to sit. His name was actually Frank but there were three or four from his area and they insisted on calling him Blooper so the name stuck. After exchanging names, Blooper said, "I saw those two funny old men in tuxes. Were they with you?" Remembering his moment of rejection of the two funny old men and still being slightly ashamed of himself, he said, "Yes, they're my great uncles and they were honoring me by wearing their best clothes." Blooper quickly looked the other way. There had been no one to see him off. He doubted if his father even cared that he was gone. He wouldn't even know it until he came out of his alcoholic fog. Joey leaned back and shut his eyes hoping to shut Blooper out, but could soon see that this was not to be. Blooper said, "Those little red headed girls- are they your sisters? What are their names? How old are they?"

Joey thought he might as well give in to it and maybe he needed to go on the offensive, and he said, "Yes, they are 8 years old and their names are Molly and Ethel Grace. My little brother is 7 and he seems to be everywhere they are. Ethel Grace wanted to marry me until I told her she was my sister and we couldn't get married."

Blooper asked, "Was she the quiet one or the one who was popping all over the place?"

"She was the popper," he answered.

"The quiet one is the prettiest,"

Joey looked at him in surprise. "They're identical twins. They look just alike."

"That's how you see them, but I see a difference."

Thinking to turn the conversation to Blooper, Joey said, "What about you? Were any of your folks there?"

"Don't have any. My old man lives up in Whoopin Holler and he's drunk all the time. He doesn't even know I enlisted. Maybe I'll write to him after I get where I'm going and tell him. He's the only family I've got."

Joey was sort of into this conversation by now and offered the information that Claudia was his girl friend and some day he hoped to marry her. Blooper looked pensive and said, "I never had a girl friend."

"Why not," Joey queried. He couldn't imagine the solitary life Blooper was portraying.

The only girl in the Holler is Carolyn Rose. Nobody knows what her last name is but she lives with Granny Dimity and some think she's her granddaughter. She's kind of dopey. I never figured any girl worth her salt would go for an ugly puss like mine." Joey turned and looked at Blooper more carefully. He had a normal sized nose, a wide mouth, thin lips, brown eyes, and ears that protruded slightly. They all seemed to be well placed and all together they made up a rather interesting face. When he smiled, everything fell into place. He decided that all Blooper needed was a friend to bolster his ego, and maybe he would amount to something. "Well," he thought, "We'll see!"

Fate seemed to keep Joey and Blooper together. In Basic Training they were billeted in the same barracks. They were both assigned to the Medical Corps, which meant extra training. In September of 1943 they were sent to England. Hitler was bombarding London with the V-2 rocket in preparation to invade. By this time they were Army buddies, and Blooper had gained a good bit of confidence. They were seen together all the time and the other men had picked up a modicum of respect for Blooper due to Joey.

Claudia had indeed been with child and just before the baby was born Joey was able to come home and he and Claudia were married. Blooper had come with him, supposedly to see his father but he spent all of his time at the Morrisons and he never did get to Whoopin Holler. Joey managed to get home in August of 1943 and see his son once before he went overseas. He was 11 months old by now and his name was Joseph Jones, Jr. The family worshipped the little boy. Claudia stayed with them as her folks had gone to Detroit to work in the war factories. She and Ruthie shared the secrets of young women; therefore Claudia was one of the first to know about Gunter Drake, formerly Von Dracht. Gunter's father had legally changed his name when Hitler's antics in Europe put Germans in a different light. He had been in high school with her and they had mutual friends. Nothing serious had happened, but now Ruthie's hormonal urges had kicked in, and when Gunter came into the menswear department at Dunsmores with his brother, he spotted Ruthie in the Bridal Section and made his way over there. Before he left, he asked if she would go to a moving picture with him Saturday night. She promptly invited him to supper at the farm and he accepted. Their relationship quickly escalated and as soon as Gunter started talking enlistment, Ruthie made up her mind that he was the one for her and set about winning a proposal of marriage from him. Yes, they were young, but with the men going off to war, young couples were anxious to get married.

Donald was strangely intrigued by the reports from Claudia's father who had gone to Detroit to work in the automobile factories when they turned to war production. Her mother wrote glowing reports of housing (quaint), wages, (fantastic), and entertainment (enjoyable). Underlying all this, Emily could sense that the woman was homesick and was trying desperately to lure Claudia and her grandson to Yankeeland. Claudia was reminded that she could also get a job there and save the money for a start when Joey came home. As it turned out, there was no need to worry. Claudia wanted to stay where Joey would come to when he had leave.

But the thought of the wages and adventure began to worm its way into Donald's mind. Ruthie and Claudia could live here on the farm with Dag and take care of things. It seemed like such a wonderful idea. He had never been much of anywhere and he didn't think Emily had either. Emily and the kids could come to Detroit with him and share the big adventure. He started talking it up to them, but to his surprise, none of them were overly enthusiastic about leaving the farm. Vernie wanted to know who would help Grandpa with the barn chores. Dag had procured another mule. He couldn't help but think that a man was not quite complete without his mule. Vernie had wanted to name her Spot to honor the old dog that had died the year before, but the girls had outvoted him and named her Jeeter. Dag had also fixed up the old sleigh from behind the barn and introduced the kids to sleigh rides.

Molly and Ethel Grace had pretty much the same arguments but they threw in the chickens and the possibility of their father coming back. Even so, they were more afraid he would come back than that he wouldn't. The Morrisons had adopted them legally so they knew they wouldn't have to go with him, but that didn't drive the uneasiness away. Emily's argument and the one that held the most weight was: "What if Joey comes home on leave and we don't get to see him? What if our grandchild doesn't know us when we get home?"

Donald secretly wondered if their old car would make it to Michigan and back. If Joey came home on leave could he get time off at the factory to come home and see him? Then there was gasoline rationing to deal with. Could he get gas to come home if something went wrong here?

In the end, Emily said, "As much as I love you, Donald, I can't do this. I see Vernies happy face at the breakfast table and wonder what it would look like at a table in the city. I would wonder all the time if my father was standing up under the strain of taking care of the farm all right. I would wonder if Claudia was about to give birth to my first grandchild. If you are so bent on doing this, you will have to go by yourself. Besides, I really doubt that Flossie Green is having such a great time as she says. As long as I have known her, she has loved to exaggerate and put a shining face on everything in <u>her</u> life. You know very well that she wants Claudia to come live with them."

Donald decided the next morning to check out the fences on the farm and make sure they were in good condition. Dag offered to help him but Donald declined. He wanted the day to himself to do some deep soul-searching. As the day progressed, he began to have niggling little doubts about his grand idea. How could I go off there and leave all the work here to Ruthie and Dag? How could I be so far from home when our boy is over there risking his life fighting for his country? How can I come home every night and not see Vernie's smiling face? How can I leave Emmy to live by herself? She has been like a gift from heaven. How can I be separated from her for so long? And this is not even to mention Molly and Ethel Grace. They're like my own children. And Grandmother who is getting up there in years- what if she should die and I wasn't here? Who knows how long Pop has got on this earth? Bear and Garr have been special gifts to us all- and I haven't even mentioned Joey's unborn baby who is so precious to us.

In late afternoon his stomach was beginning to rumble and he thought of sitting around the supper table with his family and the big adventure was seeming more like a big mistake. He put his fence-mending tools in the truck and made his way home. As he turned the motor off by the back door, he looked up to see Emily framed in the doorway. Up on the porch, he put his arms around her, and said, "I'm not going, Em." That night in bed, she turned to him and said, "I didn't know how on earth I was going to let you go." Emily slept soundly that night for the first time in 3 months.

Chapter 33

NORMANDY

There was a report of the sighting of a submarine off Cape Cod Bay- a German submarine, of course. The cities had imposed a blackout every night so they could not be seen from the air (German bombers). People in the country were honor-bound to turn off lights at night and every window in the country had blackout curtains. On the West Coast, all the Japanese born citizens were rounded up and taken to Internment Camps in the Midwest. Whether this was right or wrong, people were scared. A woman driving across the Mojave Desert suddenly began to hear broadcasts from Tokyo Rose through the fillings in her teeth. People were urged to save cooking grease, tinfoil from cigarette packages, newspapers, string, and tin cans. Nothing was to be thrown away. Rationing of canned goods, meat, sugar, and other staples was put into effect. Shoes were rationed and gasoline stamps were issued according to a person's job and how far they had to drive.

A standard joke of the times said that it took more gasoline to stop and start a car up again so carpoolers would say that they slowed down to ten miles per hour and the passenger who wanted to get out would open the door and start running when their feet hit the ground. When they picked them up at night, the routine was reversed and they started running and jumped into the car. This was told in jest, as most of the war workers were old men and women.

Women had never worked in a factory before and Rosie the Riveter became a symbol of the War Effort. Signs with pictures of Uncle Sam pointing straight at whoever was standing in front of the poster were hanging everywhere. He was saying, "Loose lips sink ships!" The government passed a law that all able-bodied men and women had to sign up to work in a War factory. But they also realized that the farmer had a big part to play in the war effort. Therefore,

Donald had signed up with the Department of Agriculture to raise certain crops for the government, so that he wouldn't find himself in Detroit against his will.

Congress had passed the Selective Training and Service Act of 1940 on September 16, 1940 so the draft was already in place when Pearl Harbor was attacked. But thousands of young men like Joey didn't wait for the draft.

Right after their leave in August 1943, Joey and Blooper were sent to England. The Germans had developed the V-2 Rocket, which could be launched from flatbed semi-trucks making them mobile and very hard to find and destroy with bombs. The rockets were 46 feet long and noiseless so no one knew they were coming until they were right on top of them. Hitler had boasted that they were going to flatten and destroy London. The British and the Russians both were in grave danger of being overrun when the United States joined the War. The men's contacts with their families now were almost all by V-mail service.

V-mail was an unusual and ingenious system for delivering mail from United States troops to home addresses. V-mail correspondence worked by photographing large amounts of censored mail and reduced to thumbnail size onto reels of microfilm, which weighed much less than the original would have. The film reels were shipped to the US, sent to prescribed destinations for developing at a receiving station near the recipient, and printed out on lightweight photo paper. These facsimiles of the letter-sheets were reproduced about one-quarter the original size and the miniature mail was delivered to the addressee.

V-mail was composed of a letter that folded into its own envelope. The user would write the message in the prescribed space, fold the letter/envelope form, address it, affix postage and then the mail was on its way.

According to the National Postal Museum, "V-mail ensured that thousands of tons of shipping space could be reserved for war materials. A single mail sack could replace the 37 mailbags required to carry 150,000 one-page letters.

In February 1944, Joey wrote this letter to his mother and a similar one to Claudia:

February 10, 1944.

Dear Mom,

As you know by now, I have to be very careful what I say or the censor's will cut this letter to pieces. We have been bombing the Hell out of the countries across the way. Some are guessing that something big is coming down but I would not venture a guess. I will just be glad when this is all over and I can come home to my wife and baby. Blooper and I are medics and we will not be carrying guns. We will be carrying medical supplies and trying to save the lives of our comrades who are struck down. I learned yesterday that Blooper and I have both made lieutenant. I love all of you and hope you all include me in your prayers every night. Say a prayer for Blooper, too, as he doesn't have anyone to pray for him. Vernie has a birthday coming up on the 20th. What will it be, Vernie, the 9th or the 19th? Happy birthday, anyway.

From your loving son, Joey

From Blooper to Molly:

February 1944

Good Golly, Miss Molly,

It seems like a hundred years since I have seen you. I carry that lucky stone you gave me in my pocket all the time. I'll bet you are as tall as I am by now. But, wait a minute, that can't be right. Joey says you are 10 years old now. How could someone who is only 10 years old make a wonderful tasting apple pie like you made the last time I was there? I look at the picture I took of the family at Thanksgiving time and wish you were truly my family. But I guess it's better late than never. Please write to me!

As ever, Frank (Blooper)

Donald to Joey:

February 1944

Dear Son,

Of course we include you in our prayers. You <u>are</u> our prayers. And we put Blooper right in there with you. Your mama thinks of you all the time. I am constantly thankful that I didn't go to Detroit to work and hope you will forgive me for not standing behind you. I have signed up for a government program to produce crops to feed the armed services. So maybe when you are eating bread you will look it over good to see if the wheat came from our farm. Ha! Ha!

From Your Papa who misses you Very Much, Donald Morrison

Molly to Blooper:

March 1944

Dear Frank,

I have decided to call you Frank because it is more dignified than Blooper. I learned what dignified meant in school and I like Frank better. Mama says that being a medic is next thing to being a doctor. Do you like to do it? I am in the 5th grade this year. Ethel Grace and I are doing an art project together for school. I don't know if I am very good at art. Ethel Grace is better but I can make a better apple pie and I will make another one for you when you come again. We say prayers for you and Joey every night. We ask God to keep you safe and bring you back home to us.

With Love from Molly Morrison

In the last week of May 1944, copies of Dwight D. Eisenhower's speech to the troops were posted at all military bases:

SOLDIERS, SAILORS AND AIRMEN OF THE ALLIED EXPEDITIONARY FORCE!

You are about to embark upon the Great Crusade, toward which we have striven these many months. The eyes of the world are upon you. The hopes and prayers of liberty-loving people everywhere march with you. In company with our brave Allies and brothers-in-arms on other Fronts, you will bring about the destruction of the German war machine, the elimination of Nazi tyranny over the oppressed peoples of Europe, and security for ourselves in a free world.

Your task will not be an easy one. Your enemy is well trained, well equipped and battle hardened. He will fight savagely.

But this is the year 1944! Much has happened since the Nazi triumphs of 1940-41. The United Nations has inflicted upon the Germans great defeats, in open battle, man-to-man. Our air offensive has seriously reduced their strength in the air and their capacity to wage war on the ground. Our Home Fronts have given us an overwhelming superiority in weapons and munitions of war, and placed at our disposal great reserves of trained fighting men. The tide has turned! The free men of the world are marching together to Victory!

I have full confidence in your courage and devotion to duty and skill in Battle. We will accept nothing less than full Victory!

Good luck! And let us beseech the blessing of Almighty God upon this great and noble undertaking.

SIGNED: Dwight D. Eisenhower

The Battle of Normandy, codenamed Operation Overlord, was the Allied invasion of Normandy, part of the Normandy Campaign. It began on June 6, 1944 (commonly known as D-Day), and is held to end on June 30, 1944, with Operation Cobra. As of 2007, Operation Overlord remains the largest sea borne invasion in history, involving over 156,000 troops crossing the English Channel from England to Normandy.

The Normandy invasion began with overnight parachute and glider landings, massive air attacks, naval bombardments, and an early morning amphibious phase began on June 6. The "D-Day" forces deployed from bases along the south coast of England, the most important of these being Portsmouth.

Elements of the 1st Infantry Division and 29th Infantry Division faced the veteran German 352nd Infantry Division, one of the best trained on the beaches. Allied intelligence failed to realize that the relatively low-quality 716th Infantry Division had been replaced by the 352nd the previous March. Omaha was also the most heavily fortified beach, with high bluffs defended by mortars, machine guns, and artillery, and the pre-landing aerial and naval bombardment of the bunkers proved to be ineffective.

Difficulties in navigation caused the majority of landings to drift eastwards, missing their assigned sectors, and the initial assault waves of tanks, infantry and engineers took heavy casualties. The official record stated, "Within 10 minutes of the ramps being lowered, [the leading] company had become inert, leaderless and almost incapable of action. Every officer and sergeant had been killed or wounded. It had become a struggle for survival and rescue". Only a few gaps were blown in the beach obstacles, resulting in problems for subsequent landings. The heavily defended draws, the only vehicular routes off the beach, could not be taken and two hours after the first assault the beach was closed for all but infantry landings. Commanders considered abandoning the beachhead, but small units of infantry, often forming improvised groups, supported by naval artillery and the surviving tanks, eventually infiltrated the coastal defenses by scaling the bluffs between strongpoints. Further infantry landings were able to exploit the initial penetrations and by the end of the day two isolated footholds had been established. American casualties at Omaha on D-Day numbered around 3,000 out of 34,000 men, most in the first few hours, whilst the defending forces suffered 1,200 killed, wounded or missing. The tenuous beachhead was expanded over the following days, and the original D-Day objectives were accomplished by D+3.

Joey and Blooper were with the 29th Infantry Division and miraculously made it to the beach on June 6. They had been tending the wounded in an out-of-the-way spot on the beach and helping with their evacuation for 2 days now, even though their company had made its way into one of the footholds farther on from the beach. They had just decided that enough medics had made it to take care of the wounded there and they could leave to find their own company. They were gathering up their supplies and Blooper said to Joey, "Do we need to take these boxes?" When he received no answer, he turned around to look and saw Joey lying across a wounded comrade with an ugly, bloody hole in his chest. He dropped to his knees beside his buddy and felt for a pulse. There was none. Partially numb from what had just happened, he next checked to make sure that Joey's dog tags were intact, and then went through his pockets and found an unfinished letter to his mother, which he confiscated. He took everything that Joey would not need any more. A bullet from a sniper's gun barely missed his head and made him aware that he needed to leave quickly as it was now imperative to store everything about Joey's death in his memory to tell to the family on another day.

On the Homefront: Every family, wealthy or poor, knew that something big was happening in Europe. The wealthy had their large 'Philco' consoles in their parlors, The middle class had their box style "Philco' in the kitchen and the poor haunted the newspaper office and 'Dunsmore's Menswear and Bridal Store' where a megaphone had been placed on the sidewalk for the very poor. Anyone who could afford the price of a ticket to the local theater was rewarded with a half hour of big screen moving pictures of the action with every movie.

The Morrisons figured that Joey and Blooper were involved in this action so, even though nerves were on edge, they were not surprised when they didn't get any letters from the boys. Like everyone with loved ones over there, 'no news was good news', so they went on about their daily routine and hoped and prayed.

On August 29, with nerves strung taut, Emily and Claudia decided to make a batch of bread. Claudia had been crying that morning and Emily thought maybe doing something useful would distract her. They had just put the loaves into pans to raise for the final time when Emily heard a can turn into the drive. Donald and Dag, working out in the field, had seen a khaki- colored car on the road going toward the farmhouse. Quickly they jumped into the truck and headed for the house. All three of them knew what this signaled. Emily, with Claudia right behind her stepped out on to the porch. Without prompting, Claudia stepped over to the dinner bell and started ringing it, forever a portent of trouble. Donald heard the bell as he came by the barn, and he knew as sure as shootin' that it was about Joey. He and Dag were on the porch almost before the truck had stopped rolling. He took in the fear on Claudia's face and the stoicism on Emily's that would carry her through most anything. Oddly enough, Dag had stationed himself at Claudia's side, even though he had never been terribly fond of her.

The two men in the car, although this was their job and they had done it many times, were loath to inform another family of the death of their loved one. They were stalling by rifling through some papers until the two men reached the porch. Only then did Lieutenant Frith and Sergeant Bloomfield from the local recruiting office alight from their car and approach the porch. He introduced himself and the sergeant and said, "Are you Emily and Donald Morrison and Claudia Morrison?" Donald gave his slight nod but Emily spoke out in a strong voice, "We are, sir, to what do we owe this visit?"

"Is your son lieutenant Joseph H. Jones of the 29th Infantry Division?"

"Yes."

"Ma'am, we regret to inform you that your son, Lieutenant Joseph H. Jones, SSN 236-89-4445 was killed on June 7, 1944 on Omaha Beach at Normandy, France. He was attending the wounded on the beach and was hit by sniper fire. We have word that his personal belongings will be returned to you by one Lieutenant Frank Adams at the first possible chance he gets. His body lies in the American cemetery in Colleville-sur-Mer at present. Upon request it will be disinterred and returned to you at the end of the hostilities."

Claudia managed a small cry and fainted at Dag's feet. He started patting her cheeks and she revived, whereupon he helped her up and took her in the house. She was a strong girl and revived when she heard little Joey awaken from his nap in the crib in the corner of the kitchen.

As the two messengers turned away, Lieutenant Frith rubbed at his eyes. He would never get accustomed to delivering these messages. And besides that, he well remembered the opening days of the Recruiting Office when everything was in a tumult and young Joey Jones had been a big help to him. He wondered if Mrs. Morrison had saved that stupid letter of commendation he had made up out of whole cloth to give to the boys that had pitched in to help him. She probably had and he hoped it would be a big comfort to her. He also hoped that she didn't find out that the President of the United States had nothing to do with it.

Donald put his arm around Emily's waist and tugged her gently toward the barn. "But I've got to see if Claudia is all right," she said. "No," Donald answered, "Dag will see to her. We need a few minutes to ourselves."

Chapter 34

VE Day

Donald didn't stop at the barn. He kept a hold on Emily's elbow like she was going to run away from him, which was the farthest thing on her mind. Actually, she had come to look at Donald as a haven of logical thinking and understanding. And besides that, she knew that he was also hurting from losing Joey. So when he turned into the field behind the barn and headed for the Big Stone, which the kids always used to mount Old Prancer, she knew why he had brought her here. The first image she saw was Joey standing on the Stone and shouting, "Look at me, Mom, I can get on by myself."

Donald boosted her up on the stone and then climbed up beside her. He snuggled up to her and put his arm around her and his kind gestures literally undid her. She began to sob and couldn't seem to stop. Before long, Donald's face was streaming tears and they were blending in with Emily's. They must have sat there silently and cried together for 15 minutes when Emily said, "We need to go to the store and get Ruthie and tell her, then go tell Pop and Grandmother, so we can be back home when Vernie and the girls get home."

"Yes," said Donald, "I'm thinking that we need to take them into a room by themselves to tell them. Do you have any idea what to say to them?"

"Well," I can't see saying too much about him being in heaven. They are too old for that to faze them much. Maybe we need to think about it beforehand and just tell them mainly the truth. Maybe we need to stress how proud we are of him, and how lucky we are to have had him for 21 years. Right now we need to get back to the house and see if Claudia is all right."

"Dag will have taken care of her. Don't you remember how comforting he can be at times? He has been a Godsend to us."

When they reached the house, they could smell the wonderful aroma of home made bread baking. Dag wanted to know if they should go with them to tell the others and Emily could see that both he and Claudia had been crying. She said she thought he should stay with Claudia and the baby, and take care of the bread, maybe even make a pot of soup as she was sure that Pop and Grandmother would be out tonight. Donald had said that none of them should be alone the first night after receiving this dreadful news.

They drove into town in silence and parked almost in front of Dunsmores store. Emily asked, "Should we both go in?" "No," Donald told her, "I'll go in and get her and then we'll all go over to Oakland St. We don't want to tell her in the store and she'll know something is wrong when she sees you've been crying." He entered the store, which had a brand new face from the first time she had seen it. Ruthie spied him when he came in the front door and went to meet him. Immediately she knew that something was wrong. "Is it Joey?" she asked. Donald just gave a slight nod of his head and said, "You need to come with us to Grandmother's house." She said a quick word to another woman working there, picked up her handbag from under the counter, and followed him out. Once outside, he put his arm around her waist and said, "Your mama is in the car. She is doing as well as can be expected, but she needs all the rest of us to be strong, too.

Ruthie and Emily climbed into the back seat. Emily wanted to hold her hand while they talked. Ruthie was trying desperately to keep the tears from starting. Emily told her about everything she could remember that the Lieutenant had told her. When she said that Blooper had been with him and taken possession of his personal items, Ruthie could no longer remain detached. She started sobbing and Emily reminded her that they had to go tell Pop and Grandmother so she needed to stop crying for now.

As the three of them went up on the porch, Vern came out the door and his intuition kicked in immediately. He had more or less been steeling himself for this moment since Pearl Harbor was bombed.

"Joey?" he asked. Donald gave his signature nod of the head, and Vern reached out his hand to Emily, then to Ruthie as he could see that she was very upset. "Come on in," he said, "Clara is taking a nap but she would never forgive me if I didn't wake her up." Clara was 83 years old now and had retired from doing anything at the store, but she had not retired from life.

He touched her shoulder and said, "The family is here and we need you out in the parlor." She asked, "Is it news of Joey?" When he said it was, she told him she would be right out. It took her about 5 minutes to perform the necessary functions and came out looking neat as a pin. One look at the company told her all she needed to know. She hugged all three of them in turn and said, "Now, tell me all about it." Emily nodded at Donald and he started the story. He told everything he could remember and Emily filled in the parts he missed. Then he said, "We have to get home before the children do. Why don't you come on out to the farm. Dag and Claudia are making something to eat tonight? We all need to be together." Vern agreed and Clara said, "I made a cake this morning. We'll bring that!"

The schoolhouse was only a mile away from the house, but Donald decided to pick the kids up at the school. When they came out looking puzzled, Donald greeted them with a smile and said that their mother was eager to see them. At home, all three of them could see that something was afoot and it made them uneasy. Claudia was crying again and Ruthie was trying to ease her grief. Grandpa Dag was strangely silent, and Emily had a strained look on her face. She said, "You children go change your clothes and Papa and I will be right up to talk to you in your room." Ethel Grace, ever the agitator, said, "Don't you want us to do our chores first?" Donald answered, "They can wait a bit."

Ten minutes later, Emily knocked on Vernie's door, and bade him to come into the girl's room. The three of them sat in a row on the bed and Donald pulled a chair away from the desk for Emily. He waited for her to begin. In her usual stoic manner, she told them the only way she knew how-truthfully. She said, "We had a couple of visitors today. They were from the United States Government Office. They had news of Joey. He died in the big battle at Normandy last month. Blooper was with him and I expect we'll be hearing from him as soon as he has time."

There was a moment of silence and Ethel Grace said, "I suppose this means we'll never see him again. He won't be coming home, will he?"

Vernie, who was crying by now said, "Joey said he'd teach me to ride his bicycle when he got home. Who's going to help me now?"

Molly, who was also crying, said, "Did Blooper get hurt? When will he be coming to see us?"

Emily tried to answer all three, "No, he won't be coming home again. We just have to remember the good times with him and be glad we had him for as long as we did. You see, when God gives children to us, it isn't forever. It's for as long as we need to take care of them and make good people out of them. Sometimes we have them for a very long time and sometimes not long enough. And, Vernie, as far as the bicycle is concerned, you still have Papa and Ruthie and me to help you learn. And, Molly, I don't know about Blooper, but I'd stake my last dollar that we will be seeing him after the War is over. He will tell us all about it then. You can go do your chores now. If there is anything else you want to talk about, any of us will be glad to talk to you. Pops and Grandmother are coming out tonight and I'm sure that Grandpa Dag has called Uncle Bear and Uncle Garr, so I look for them to come driving in any minute. Just one word of caution! Claudia is very upset, so be careful what you say to her. She needs some extra consideration right now." As they left the room, Donald took her hand and said, "That was marvelous! I couldn't have done it better."

American War Mothers

In 1917 Army Captain Robert L. Queissner of the 5th Ohio Infantry designed and patented a simple flag to reflect the World War I service of two sons. The appeal of this flag quickly caught on, and on September 24, 1917, an Ohio congressman read into the <u>Congressional Record</u>:

"The world should know of those who give so much for liberty. The dearest thing in all the world to a father and mother — their children."

Three days later the American War Mothers organized in Indiana, and that organization quickly grew in other states. It was a close-knit group, composed of women with one thing in common...a child at risk because of their choice to answer their Nation's call to military service. Throughout the war, these mothers displayed a flag with a blue star in their window, denoting the service of a son or daughter. When World War I began claiming the lives of many of these young Americans, a new flag developed. When a son was killed in action a GOLD star was sewn over the blue one, completely covering it. In May 1918 the Women's Committee of National Defenses suggested to President Woodrow Wilson that those mothers who had lost a family member in the war should wear a black band on their upper-left arm, adorned with a gold star. In a letter affirming his support for this proposal, President Wilson referred to these women as *"Gold Star Mothers"*. It was the beginning of a new tradition of patriotic support for those who serve our Nation in uniform.

As Vern and Clara entered the house later that afternoon, he handed Emily a package from Dunsmores. In it was a small window flag with a Gold Star in the middle of it. Emily quickly took down the Blue Star flag and replaced it with the Gold Star. She handed it to Claudia, saying, "Save this for little Joey. He will cherish it some day."

Ruthie and Gunter

September 1, 1944

Dear Gunter,

Last Thursday we received word that Joey had been killed by sniper fire on Omaha Beach on the second day of the battle. Blooper was with him and when he gets home, he will tell us more of the facts, although I'm not sure how many more facts there can be. The main thing is that Joey is not coming home, and I will never see my beloved brother again. Claudia is distraught but she says how glad she is that they were married and she has little Joey. My mother is a very strong person and when someone in town asks her about Joey, you can literally see her spine stiffen and her jaw set and she tries to answer all of their questions. Running out of room here! I have to ask you something. Before you are shipped overseas, will you marry me? I know we are both young but we do love each other and it would kill me if anything happened to you and we hadn't taken this step.

All my love, Ruthie

September 25, 1944

Dear Ruthie,

YES! YES! YES! I don't care if we have a wedding or just go down to the courthouse. I feel sure that I will be sent overseas as soon as I have had a leave. What will your folks say? I think it will be all right with mine as they like you pretty much. So go ahead and make any plans you have to just so they don't take up too much of my leave. I love you with all my heart.

Gunter

By the first week in November, Gunter was home on leave and Ruthie had plans all in place to have a small wedding at the Methodist Church in town on a Friday night two days after he arrived home. She had even arranged to rent a white wedding gown from Dunsmore's Bridal Shoppe. After a small reception put on by the Methodist ladies, the two of them departed for a week-end at the same hotel where Donald and Emily had spent their wedding (commitment) night.

Before Gunter left, they had worked out a plan. He felt sure that he would be sent to a fighting zone, so he told her to listen to the news and he would start his letter to her with the first letter of the place he was shipped to. Everyone was dispensing with 'Dear___' to save space on the V-Mail. So if he landed in Germany, he would start with 'Great!' or if it was China, he would say 'Cause I love you', so she needed to pay attention to the news and watch the first word of his letters. It was quite an ingenuous plan even though he suspected that others had some kind of a plan worked out. He told her if the censors caught on and started blanking out the first word they would change to the 5th word. Thereby, they had laid a basis for keeping track of where Gunter was in the world. Ruthie thought it would be some measure of comfort. Little did she know it would also be a source of great stress.

~~~~~~~~~~~~~~~

BATTLE of the BULGE
December 16, 1944 to January 25, 1945

On 16 December 1944 the Germans started their *ARDENNES OFFENSIVE*. The 106th Infantry Division, in place on a salient jutting out into Germany was hit with full force. After three days of battle, two of the Regiments, the 422nd and the 423rd were surrounded. The 424th, south of the other two regiments, was able to withdraw and join with the 112th Regiment of the 28th Infantry Division. They formed a Regimental Combat Team and were successful in the oncoming days of January 1945 in helping counter the German attack driving the Germans back through the same area where the 106th had been in position in mid-December 1944. This German Offensive became known in the U.S. Forces journals as *The Battle of the Bulge.*

On a wintry mid-December day in 1944, three powerful German armies plunged into the semi-mountainous, heavily forested Ardennes region of eastern Belgium and northern Luxembourg. Their goal was to reach the sea, trap four allied armies, and impel a negotiated peace on the Western front.

Thinking the Ardennes was the least likely spot for a German offensive, American Staff Commanders chose to keep the line thin, so that the manpower might concentrate on offensives north and south of the Ardennes. The American line was thinly held by three divisions and a part of a fourth, while the fifth was making a local attack and a sixth was in reserve. Division sectors were more than double the width of normal, defensive fronts.

Even though the German Offensive achieved total surprise, nowhere did the American troops give ground without a fight. Within three days, the determined American stand and the arrival of powerful reinforcements insured that the ambitious German goal was far beyond reach.

In snow and sub-freezing temperatures the Germans fell short of their interim objective - that of reaching the sprawling Meuse River on the fringe of the Ardennes. All the Germans accomplished was to create a Bulge in the American line. In the process they expended irreplaceable men, tanks and material. Four weeks later, after grim fighting, with heavy losses on both the American and German sides, the Bulge ceased to exist.

Battle Action Credits: The 106th Infantry Division was credited with a holding action that used much of the precious time of the German Offensive. Time was an important and vital ingredient in Hitler's plan to break through to the Meuse River and then to go for Antwerp. The first three days of battle were vital and the 106th Infantry Division slowed his advance in the St. Vith area. By doing so the 106th played a large role in the final defeat of the German Army. The delay and extended battle used so much of the precious resources of the German Army that they were never again able to recoup and fight the style of war they had in earlier days. This delay in time was a big key in the final downfall of the German plans for their *ARDENNES OFFENSIVE.* The loss of their resources, both human and equipment accelerated their final defeat and caused an early end to the long war in Europe.

~~~~~~~~~~~~~~~~

Ruthie received a V-Mail from Gunter the first week in January and he started out, "Boy, do I miss you!" She had already had one letter from him that started "106 reasons to love you". She hadn't yet figured out the first one, so she brought up the subject at the supper table, and told about their code. Donald said, "Have you been listening to the news? It's all over the 'Philco' that the 106th Infantry Division is engaging in a fierce battle in Germany now." At Ruthie's worried look, Donald wished he hadn't given out so much information. But the fat was in the fire now and he knew she wouldn't let go of it. "But he's somewhere beginning with a B," she said. "The news will be on in half an hour," Dag put in, "We'll see where the 106th is fighting."

The women hurried to get the kitchen cleaned up so they could be quiet when the news came on. Even the children stayed in the kitchen to hear what was happening over there.

~~~~~~~~~~~~~~~~~

The reporter announced that tonight Ernie Pyle, a renowned war reporter who was currently covering the Battle of the Bulge would be giving us the news on that front: (The following was taken from Ernie Pyle's column he wrote for newspapers right on site at the battlefield.)

A Slow Cautious Business

ON THE WESTERN FRONT, December 1944 - I know that all of us correspondents have tried time and again to describe to you what this weird hedgerow fighting in northwestern France has been like.

But I'm going to go over it once more, for we've been in it two months and some of us feel that this is the two months that broke the German Army in the west. This type of fighting is always in small groups, so let's take as an example one company of men. Let's say they are working forward on both sides of a country lane, and this company is responsible for clearing the two fields on either side of the road as it advances.

That means you have only about one platoon to a field. And with the company's understrength from casualties, you might have no more than twenty-five or thirty men in a field.

Over here the fields are usually not more than fifty yards across and a couple of hundred yards long. They may have grain in them, or apple trees, but mostly they are just pastures of green grass, full of beautiful cows.

The fields are surrounded on all sides by immense hedgerows, which consist of an ancient earthen bank, waist-high, all matted with roots, and out of which grow weeds, bushes, and trees up to twenty feet high. The Germans have used these barriers well. They put snipers in the trees. They dig deep trenches behind the hedgerows and cover them with timber, so that it is almost impossible for artillery to get at them.

Sometimes they will prop up machine guns with strings attached, so they can fire over the hedge without getting out of their holes. They even cut out a section of the hedgerow and hide a big gun or a tank in it, covering it with brush.

Also they tunnel under the hedgerows from the back and make the opening on the forward side just large enough to stick a machine gun through.

But mostly the hedgerow pattern is this: a heavy machine gun hidden at each end of the field and infantrymen hidden all along the hedgerow with rifles and machine pistols.

*

Now it's up to us to dig them out of there. It's a slow and cautious business, and there is nothing very dashing about it. Our men don't go across the open fields in dramatic charges such as you see in the movies. They did at first, but they learned better.

They go in tiny groups, a squad or less, moving yards apart and sticking close to the hedgerows on either side of the field. They creep a few yards, squat, wait, then creep again.

If you could be right up there between the Germans and the Americans you wouldn't see very many men at any one time - just a few here and there, always trying to keep hidden. But you would hear an awful lot of noise.

Our men were taught in training not to fire until they saw something to fire at. But that hasn't worked in this country, because you see so little. So the alternative is to keep shooting constantly at the hedgerows. That pins the Germans in their holes while we sneak up on them.

The attacking squads sneak up the sides of the hedgerows while the rest of the platoon stay back in their own hedgerow and keep the forward hedge saturated with bullets. They shoot rifle grenades too, and a mortar squad a little farther back keeps lobbing mortar shells over onto the Germans.

The little advance groups get up to the far ends of the hedgerows at the corners of the field. They first try to knock out the machine guns at each corner. They do this with hand grenades, rifle grenades and machine guns.

Usually, when the pressure gets on, the German defenders of the hedgerow start pulling back. They'll take their heavier guns and most of the men back a couple of fields and start digging in for a new line.

They leave about two machine guns and a few riflemen scattered through the hedge, to do a lot of shooting and hold up the Americans as long as they can.

Our men now sneak along the front side of the hedgerow, throwing grenades over onto the other side and spraying the hedges with their guns. The fighting is very close - only a few yards apart - but it is seldom actual hand-to-hand stuff.

Sometimes the remaining Germans come out of their holes with their hands up. Sometimes they try to run for it and are mowed down. Sometimes they won't come out at all, and a hand grenade, thrown into their hole, finishes them off.

And so we've taken another hedgerow and are ready to start on the one beyond.

This hedgerow business is a series of little skirmishes like that clear across the front, thousands and thousands of little skirmishes. No single one of them is very big. But add them all up over the days and weeks and you've got a man-sized war, with thousands on both sides being killed.

~~~~~~~~~~~~~~~~

Ruthie's white face stood out in the little group of people gathered in the Morrison kitchen. She said, in little more than a whisper, "Oh, Lord' this has got to be where Gunter is." Molly said, "I wonder if Frank is there, too." Donald said, "It's where the action is. I think we can safely assume it's where they are. I'm not sure that we're better off for knowing, but since we do, we have to bite the bullet and accept it."

The Battle of the Bulge officially ended when two American forces met up on January 15, 1945. It had lasted only one month but some of the fiercest fighting of the war had occurred there.

Everybody was overjoyed when first Molly and then Ruthie received a V-Mail from Frank and Gunter, respectively, within a few days of each other. They couldn't say much about the battle but each stated that they were all in one piece. Donald and Dag privately wondered if the fighting was almost over. The news did not forbode anything wonderful for the Germans, but they also had to admit that if things were going bad for the Allies they probably wouldn't hear about it.

Gunter and Frank were not together but they were each advancing toward Berlin. Frank kept on writing to Molly and everyone wondered but nobody said much. His letters were always like 'brother' letters and Molly shared them freely with everyone else. Gunter's letters stopped coming in March and Ruthie was quietly going out of her mind. Then she received a telegram from the United States Government. Gunter had been wounded and was in an Army hospital in Germany. They gave her an address to write to, and she sent a V-mail off promptly.

On May 8th 1945 Victory in Europe was declared and there were scenes of jubilation up and down the United Kingdom. There were street parties in most towns. Thousands of people gathered in Trafalgar Square. Rations that had been saved up for this special time were brought out and there were sandwiches and cakes galore, special to the nations' children, who had been starved of sweets and treats.

On that date, massive celebrations took place, notably in London, where over a million people celebrated in a carnival atmosphere the end of the European war, though rationing of food and clothing was to continue for a number of years. In London crowds massed in particular in Trafalgar Square and up The Mall to Buckingham Palace, where King George VI and Queen Elizabeth, accompanied by the Prime Minister, Winston Churchill, appeared on the balcony of the Palace to cheering crowds. Princess Elizabeth (the future Queen Elizabeth II) and her sister Princess Margaret were allowed to wander anonymously among the crowds and take part in the celebrations in London.

May 1945

Hopefully you will remember who I am. Ruthie. I was wounded on March 6 by sniper fire. Even though the war was over, there were little pockets of Resistance here and there. If you will notice the first letter of my message, I am in the hospital. I was in a coma for 3 weeks. I am on the mend but have a scar a quarter inch deep across my left cheek about half an inch below my eye. I will no longer be a contender for Mr. America. The only ones who had time to write a letter for me were the German girls who are like Candy Stripers at home, and what they wrote, you would never have made any sense of. I'm sorry because I know you must have been going out of your mind. The doc tells me that I will be transported to the States to a military hospital in a week or so, so don't bother to write to me here. I will let you know and you can come where I am.

All my love, Gunter

Chapter 35

VICTORY OVER JAPAN

June1945, To Mrs. Gunter Drake:

We are pleased to inform you that Lieutenant Gunter Drake will be transported to Womack Army Medical Center at Fort Bragg, North Carolina on June 10, 1945. We are sending a list of housing for families of wounded men. To make a reservation or if you have any questions call 832- 999-1010 for Adjutant Kenneth Boyer.

Sincerely, Adjutant Kenneth Boyer.

June 5, 1945

Dearest Ruthie,

I will be on home turf on June 10, but will not be able to kiss the ground like I will feel like doing. I will call you as soon as I am able to reach a telephone. Love! Love! Love!

Gunter

Ruthie read both of the letters at the supper table that night, then said, "I don't know what to do. Should I wait until I hear from Gunter or should I call this adjutant? What if his plane don't get in when it's supposed to? I've never done anything like this on my own. Mama, do you think I can do it by myself?"

Emily said, "Ruthie, you're a grownup married lady now. Of course you can do it by yourself."

Donald said, "What are you sitting around here wasting time for? Get yourself some new clothes and a new suitcase and start packing."

Dag, who had been spending a lot of time in the wood shop out in the barn, got up from the table and went out toward the barn. When he came back in, he was holding something in his hand behind his back. Almost shyly, he held something out to Ruthie wrapped in a piece of tissue paper. In it was a wooden carving of a mule about 4 inches tall and Ruthie knew instinctively that it was Old Prancer. She also knew that she could receive no higher mark of respect from Dag than a present involving the old mule. "I been makin' this out in the wood shop. I was usin' the carving tools that I gave to Vern and Donald the first Christmas that you folks was here." Ruthie took note of the fine workmanship on the mule, and Dag said, "I used to do a lot of this kind of thing when I was younger. Didn't know if I could do it any more or not. I guess I did it good enough!"

Ruthie threw her arms around her grandfather and hugged him tightly.

The next morning she went into town and spent $30 of her savings on a new wardrobe and another $7 on a suitcase. She called the adjutant and had him make a reservation at a rooming house near the hospital. She could get on the train in Perryville and zip right into Fort Bragg. She decided that she would go on the 8th of June and be all settled in when Gunter's plane landed.

~~~~~~~~~~~~~~~~

September 1945

Miss Molly,

I am looking forward to seeing you. You must be 11 years old now. I hope you let the rest of the family see my letters as I write to you more than to any of the others. I am stationed in Berlin at the moment, but have been working since the end of the war with the Displaced Persons Team. At first, I was involved in the rescue of Jews in the Concentration Camps. They were a pathetic sight. There were hardly any that weighed over 90 pounds, some as little as 65. We had to carry some out, as they couldn't navigate on their own. Now we have set up a center for them all to register so that if they have any family or friends left, they may be able to find them. There were 3 Nazis in here yesterday trying to pass themselves off as Jews so they could get some of the benefits the Jews are being offered. I think they had more sinister plans in mind, as some of them really hate the Jews. Not to worry, though, they are sitting in prison today along with their fellow criminals. Word is going around among the German people here that Hitler is not dead, he is just in hiding. They are almost ready to riot as they hate him and want him dead. Military police are rounding up all of the chain of command of Hitler's regime so they can stand trial as War Criminals. I don't know when I will be sent back to the States. I have been wondering what I will do with my life after I get home. One of the possibilities is that I will make a career of the military, but I don't know yet.

As Ever, Your Friend, Frank Adams

Victory over Japan Day

(V-J day) is the celebration of the Surrender of Japan, which was initially announced on August 15, 1945 (August 14 North American date), ending combat in the Second World War. A formal Surrender happened on September 2nd.

Events leading up to the surrender

July 26, 1945: Potsdam Declaration is issued. Truman tells Japan, "Surrender or suffer prompt and utter destruction."
July 29: Japan rejects the Potsdam Declaration.
August 2: Potsdam conference ends.
August 6: An atomic bomb, "Little Boy" is dropped on Hiroshima.
August 8: USSR declares war on Japan.
August 9: Another atomic bomb, "Fat Man" is dropped on Nagasaki.
August 15: Japan surrenders.

~~~~~~~~~~~~~~~~

Japan Surrender Document

"We, acting by command of and on behalf of the Emperor of Japan, the Japanese Government and the Japanese Imperial General Headquarters, hereby accept the provisions in the declaration issued by the heads of the Governments of the United States, China, and Great Britain 26 July 1945 at Potsdam, and subsequently by the Union of Soviet Socialist Republics, which four powers are hereafter referred to as the Allied Powers.

"We hereby proclaim the unconditional surrender to the Allied Powers of the Japanese Imperial General Headquarters and of all Japanese Armed Forces and all Armed Forces under Japanese control wherever situated.

"We hereby command all Japanese forces wherever situated and the Japanese people to cease hostilities forthwith, to preserve and save from damage all ships, aircraft, and military and civil property, and to comply with all requirements which may be imposed by the Supreme Commander for the Allied Powers or by agencies of the Japanese Government at his direction.

"We hereby command the Japanese Imperial General Headquarters to issue at once orders to the commanders of all Japanese forces and all forces under Japanese control wherever situated to surrender unconditionally themselves and all forces under their control.

"We hereby command all civil, military, and naval officials to obey and enforce all proclamations, orders, and directives deemed by the Supreme Commander for the Allied Powers to be proper to effectuate this surrender and issued by him or under his authority; and we direct all such officials to remain at their posts and to continue to perform their non-combatant duties unless specifically relieved by him or under his authority.

"We hereby undertake for the Emperor, the Japanese Government, and their successors to carry out the provisions of the Potsdam Declaration in good faith, and to issue whatever orders and take whatever action may be required by the Supreme Commander for the Allied Powers or by any other designated representative of the Allied Powers for the purpose of giving effect to that declaration.

"We hereby command the Japanese Imperial Government and the Japanese Imperial General Headquarters at once to liberate all Allied Prisoners of War and civilian internees now under Japanese control and to provide for their protection, care, maintenance, and immediate transportation to places as directed.

"The authority of the Emperor and the Japanese Government to rule the State shall be subject to the Supreme Commander for the Allied Powers, who will take such steps as he deems proper to effectuate these terms of surrender".

Signed of TOKYO BAY, JAPAN of 09.04 on the SECOND day of SEPTEMBER, 1945

Mamoru Shigemitsu By Command and in behalf of the Emperor of Japan and the Japanese Government

Yoshijiro Umezu By Command and in behalf of the Japanese Imperial General Headquarters

Accepted at TOKYO BAY, JAPAN at 0908 on the SECOND day of SEPTEMBER 1945, for the United States, Republic of China, United Kingdom and the Union of Soviet Socialist Republics, and in the interests of the other United Nations at war with Japan.

Douglas MacArthur

Supreme Commander for the Allied Powers-C.W. Nimitz-United States Representative

Chapter 36

VJ DAY, AUGUST 15, 1945

The day started out like any other. Donald and Dag had gone to the field to work, and taken Vernie with them. He was growing taller by leaps and bounds, and was quite a bit of help to the men. The girls were cleaning up the house for the day and Emily and Claudia were out on the back porch getting ready to start the weekly washing. Emily saw the sun reflect light onto the side of the house and looked down the road. "What on earth is the matter with Pops?" she said and thought immediately of Clara. He was in his 1942 blue Chevrolet sedan and she had not seen him drive so fast since he lost his hand. He had barely stopped the car beside the house when he tumbled out, shouting, "IT'S OVER! IT'S OVER! THE WAR IS OVER!" He ran to the end of the porch and started ringing the dinner bell, a certain portent of trouble to those out in the fields. He kept ringing until the truck appeared around the corner of the barn with the men in it.

Donald ran up to the porch. "What's happening here, Pops?" he asked. Vern quit ringing the bell and said. "The war is over, son, and there's gonna be big doins' in town today. All of the church bells are ringing and there is a parade formin' around the fountain. Let's all go and join them now, as there will be a lot of drinkin 'and carousing' later. All of you get yourselves into my car and we'll go in and see what's goin' on." Dag made a quick telephone call to the brothers and Bear said they would join them at Sadie's Diner at 1 o'clock. Claudia declined at first, saying she would do the washing while they were gone. But Emily would have none of that. She said, "Little Joey needs to go, even if he won't remember any of it. He needs to help celebrate the thing that took his father away from him. You can tell him about it when he gets older, but he needs to be there now. Let's go change our dresses, and you girls change yours and see to it your hair is brushed. We don't want to look like a bunch of heathen. You, too, Vernie!"

Donald came in and made a pretense of sprucing himself up, but Dag disappeared into the barn. Knowing how much Vern disliked driving, Donald got into the driver's seat. Emily, Vern, and Vernie got into the car, but Claudia wanted to drive the truck in case she needed to bring Joey home early. The girls were going with her but where was Dag? Didn't he want to go? Then the barn door opened and he came out with Jeeter's new straw hat (with earholes) and an old towel in his hand. Vern had given him the hat for Christmas last year and now he said, "Does Jeeter like her hat?" He was pretty sure about why the hat was coming with them, but was not going to let on that it was anything out of the ordinary. He continued, "She does seem to be a little more sweet-tempered than Old Prancer." Dag grinned from ear to ear, as he said, "Ain't no such thing as a sweet-tempered mule A mule is a mule is a mule," Everybody laughed as he stuffed the towel into the hat and put it on his head.

When they reached Clara's house, they all squeezed into the Chevy and went down to join the parade.

There was a large fountain that was lighted at night down at the end of Main Street and the parade had originally formed in the circle around it, but it had quickly outgrown that route and as more cars joined in, they began to move eastward as far as necessary, around the block and back westward on Main Street to the fountain. Everyone was tooting the horn on their cars, people were leaning out the windows, shouting and waving. Some cars were dragging old bedsprings, tin cans, and anything that would make a lot of noise. One had a milk can tied on behind. Emily could only imagine what the man of the house was going to say when he couldn't find his milk can. Or maybe it was the man of the house driving and he had been drinking too much of his own 'shine'.

Round and round they went with the route lengthening almost every time they got to the end of it. It was almost 1 o'clock and they were headed back toward the fountain when Donald spied the Packard 8 coming toward them in the other lane. As they passed, the occupants of the Chevy all gaped. Sitting side by side in the front seat were two old men dressed in tuxedoes, white ties, and top hats. Bear was driving and Garr had his hand firmly affixed to the Klaxon horn mounted in the middle of the windshield. "OOO-GAH! OOO-GAH!, it said. Claudia was making some strangling sounds and Emily turned to her, "What's the matter?" Not to worry, she was laughing so hard she couldn't say anything coherent. Finally she said, "Did you see that? The Uncles look like they are going to the Spring Ball." Soon everyone was laughing, and Vern said, "Well, they started the war in tuxedoes and By Cracky! They're going to end it in tuxedoes."

In retrospect, Emily couldn't remember when she had seen Claudia so tickled about anything; Certainly not since Joey had died, and the gayety couldn't be anything but good.

A half hour later they heard the Klaxon right behind them going "OOO-GAH! OOO-GAH!" They stopped at the Standard Station on Grant St. the next time around. The gas gauge was getting near empty and Vern had to spend some of his precious gasoline stamps. Emily suspected that half of the people out that day had hidden hordes of gasoline and the other half would be walking everywhere for a month. The brothers pulled in behind them and Garr said, "I need a helping hand on the Klaxon horn. My hand is getting crampy." Vernie jumped up and down and shouted, "ME! ME! ME!" So Vernie and the girls got into the Packard 8 along with Dag and each one of the kids had a turn on the Klaxon.

The parade wasn't the only show in town, either. The spectators were a show of their own. Knowing that they wouldn't be in the parade, some of them had dressed in outlandish costumes, some had musical instruments, women and children were standing on the curb beating on pots and pans with large spoons, and one group had made a human ring around someone's front yard and there were half a dozen couples dancing. More and more people were getting soused to the gills, mostly on home made 'shine'. Some had brought food and were having picnics in various places up and down the 'gut' One old woman had picked every flower in her garden and was throwing them at the cars. People in the cars were trying to catch them. Four grown men were pushing an old car that had given out or run out of gas, trying to get it out of the way.

At 3 o'clock Donald said, "I'm getting hungry. Do you know we haven't eaten since breakfast?" Vern was thoughtful for a minute and then said, "I told Clara not to fuss over food today. We'll stop at Byerly's Grocery and get some hot dogs and buns and maybe some pork and beans and fix it at the house. The kids would probably like some potato chips. How does that sound?" Donald spoke up and said, "Yeah, potato chips sounds fine." Everybody was so tired it sounded good- and easy. After they had eaten, they decided to call it a day. There were chores to do back at the farm. Clara declined Vern's offer to take her downtown. She said, "I saw a mouse in the pantry this morning. I've already had my excitement for the day."

That night when they were in bed, Donald said, "What a day! Only one thing would have made it better."

"Yes," said Emily, "if Joey was with us." After a few minutes of quiet and Donald thought she had gone to sleep, she added, "I'd allow as how maybe we can get on with our lives now."

Chapter 37

AFTERMATH, 1946

The **G.I. Bill** (officially titled the **Servicemen's Readjustment Act** of 1944, PL345) provided for college or vocational education for returning World War II veterans (commonly referred to as GIs or G.I.s) as well as one year of unemployment compensation. It also provided loans for returning veterans to buy homes and start businesses.

Largely written and proposed as an omnibus bill by Warren Atherton (1891-1976), the G.I. Bill is considered to be the last piece of New Deal legislation. However, the bill, which President Franklin D. Roosevelt initially proposed, was not as far reaching. The G.I. Bill was created to prevent a repeat of the Bonus March of 1932 and a relapse into the Great Depression after World War II ended. The American Legion (a veterans group) is essentially responsible for many of the bill's provisions. The Legion, led by Atherton, managed to have the bill apply to all who served in the armed services, including African-Americans and women.

Congress failed to include merchant marine veterans in the G.I. Bill even though they are considered military personnel in times of war in accordance with the Merchant Marine Act of 1936. Merchant mariners took higher casualties than many military units (1 in 24 perished of the 215,000 who served). [1] Now that the youngest veterans are in their 80's there are efforts to finally recognize their contribution by giving some benefits to the remaining survivors. There is a pending bill in Congress. As he signed the GI Bill in June 1944 President Roosevelt said: *"I trust Congress will soon provide similar opportunities to members of the merchant marine who have risked their lives time and time again during war for the welfare of their country."*

The fact that the G.I. Bill paid for a G.I.'s entire education had encouraged many universities across the country to expand enrollment. For example, the

University of Michigan had fewer than 10,000 students prior to the war. In 1948 their enrollment was well over 30,000. Syracuse University also embraced the spirit of the Bill and saw their enrollment skyrocket from approximately 6,000 before the war to 19,000 students in 1947.

Another provision was known as the 52–20 clause. This enabled all former servicemen to receive $20 once a week for 52 weeks a year while they were looking for work. Less than 20 percent of the money set aside for the 52–20 Club (as it was known) was distributed. Rather, most returning servicemen quickly found jobs or pursued higher education.

An important provision of the G.I. Bill was low interest, zero down payment home loans for servicemen. This enabled millions of American families to move out of urban apartments and into suburban homes. Prior to the war the suburbs tended to be the homes of the wealthy and upper class. Although black servicemen were eligible for these loans they tended to remain in the inner cities or in rural areas because many suburban communities using racial segregation did not sell homes to African-Americans and other minorities.

The bill helped to democratize the "American Dream" primarily for white Americans. The G.I. Bill of Rights has since been modified but still partially remains.

It was November of 1946. Most of the men who had fought in the war were home. Wheel chairs and men on crutches were seen on the street and in church. There was a lack of housing for the new families that had formed during the war. New subdivisions of 2 and 3 bedroom houses began to spring up in the cities, many of them were cheap and shoddy. They sold like hotcakes because people were desperate for places to live. Women were asked to leave their jobs in the factories so the returning men would have employment. Some of the women were happy to return to a woman's life, but the ones who had been left to support families fought for their right to keep a job. They pretty much won. The factories that had been producing war products for four years turned back to making peacetime goods.

Thanks to the War, advances in medicine were fantastic. No longer did one have to suffer with strep throat, or Quinzy, as some had called it, until it wore itself out, sometimes damaging the heart. Before the war, aspirin had been the 'miracle drug'. Now, there was sulfa and penicillin.

New cars began to appear on the streets with a streamlined look that had never graced the automotive industry before. One of the first new models out in 1946 was the Studebaker and it was so different, it looked like it came from another planet. People dropped whatever they were doing and ran to the curb to gape at this marvelous machine. A city bus in a metropolitan area, full of people going home from work all crowded to one side of the bus to see a Studebaker on the street beside the bus. The bus driver had to yell at them to sit down before they tipped the bus over.

New and marvelous home appliances began to grace department store windows. Iceboxes were replaced by electric refrigerators. Food supplies were plentiful and rationing was coming to an end.

The old Byerly Grocery Store where the woman had to stand at the counter and tell the clerk what she wanted was seeing its last days. A large new store called 'The Market Basket' opened up on the edge of town. It had a huge parking lot, and the food was all laid out within easy reach of the customer. And, Lordy! Lordy! There were four-wheeled wire baskets called carts to wheel around through the aisles and put purchases in, before going through the cashier lane to pay for them. Last, but not least, the first of the Baby Boomers were born.

Clara, who was now 85 years old, was winding down right before Vern's eyes. It was predicted that some day people would live to be a hundred years old. In reality, 85 was almost enough for Clara. She was tired physically, tired of changes, tired of the war, food didn't taste particularly good, and she had a hard time remembering things. Many times she had thanked God that she had a son-in-law who was willing to come and live with her, sparing her the effort of living with strangers.

Vern, who was 65 years old and still managing Dunsmore Stores was looking forward to a day when someone else in the family would step up to the plate and take his place. He rather thought that Ruthie might be the one. She had worked there since she graduated and had shown a real skill in handling business affairs. Gunter had come home from the war and was working, at least temporarily in the menswear department. He and Clara had discussed having the young couple move in with them in the big house.

On this Tuesday morning he came downstairs and could not smell coffee brewing. Coffee was always Clara's contribution to breakfast. However, the kitchen was empty. Vern went to the new fridge and removed the makings for bacon and eggs. Then it struck him that there was no sound of anyone else in the house. He walked down the hall to Clara's room and tapped on the door. When there was no response, he opened the door and went in. Clara was in bed but didn't move. Nor did she move when he laid his hand on her shoulder. She had died peacefully in her sleep.

Vern called Donald and asked him to come in. Truthfully, he was feeling a bit unwound. Donald called the Beck Funeral Home and they promptly came to the house on Oakland Street to remove her. Simon Beck told them to come in at 3 o'clock and bring clothes they wanted her to be buried in.

Emily had come in and picked out suitable clothes and the three of them met with Simon at 3 o'clock. He said, "I have been doing a little research here and I see that there is a place right beside Floyd for her. You did know, didn't you, that Floyd bought a plot for 6 graves?" Donald nodded his head slightly and Vern said, "Yes, a place for me beside Flora and a place for Donald and Emily." They went through all the details about day, time, music, and minister. When asked if someone would go to the front and give a eulogy, Donald surprised the other two by saying that he would like to do it. Simon then said,

"One more thing, we need to go upstairs to the casket room so you can pick out a casket."

On the way home, Emily asked, "What are you going to say about your grandmother, Donald?" She could hardly imagine him doing something so bold. Donald answered her, "Oh, I don't know. I imagine that something will come to me." They drove a mile or so in silence, and he said, "Actually, I was hoping you would help me. I just volunteered because it wouldn't look right if somebody didn't do it, and who is there besides me? Pops is about to fall apart." Emily stared at him in amazement, and wondered who this man she had married really was. She decided that she really shouldn't be surprised by anything about him by now.

Bear and Garr came the next morning with their clothing bag they carried their tuxedoes in. "Stands to reason," said Donald. However, when they came into the kitchen, with worried looks on their faces, Dag asked them what was the matter. Garr said, "We don't hardly think it's right to wear a tuxedo to a funeral, especially one for such a nice, proper lady." "That's all the dress-up clothes we have," said Bear. "Well," Dag said, "What do you want to do about it?" Vern spoke up then, "Do you want to go down to the store and get something more appropriate?" They allowed as how they would like to do that, and the four men left in Vern's Chevy.

Three hours later, they came back, and the people in the house were speechless. Bear and Garr were both loaded down with packages and Vern had a stunned look on his face. Not, only that, but Dag also had a fair amount of purchases. If Emily wasn't mistaken, he had a garment bag, too. The twins and Dag went on into the bedroom and started opening the packages and Vern said, "They bought a little bit of everything in the store. They even bought some of that men's cologne that we got in yesterday. They wouldn't buy new shoes. They said the ones they had for their tuxes were perfectly good. They spent near $200, and Dag shucked out money for a new suit, shirt and shoes. The brothers told him that he could use some of their cologne" Emily stunned him even further by saying that maybe she and the children should have some new clothes. "We can't be the ugly ducklings," she said.

Emily and Donald had gone over some of the things he could say about his grandmother and he hoped he wouldn't get 'stage fright' and make a fool of himself. When the preacher gave him the signal, he arose from his seat. As he stood at the lectern, He looked out over the congregation, and suddenly a feeling of ease washed over him. Heck, he knew these people. He had talked to all of them at one time or another. He cleared his throat and began speaking. "My grandmother was a refined, sophisticated lady. She was born in 1861, another time. She was the daughter of a plantation owner in Virginia whose family lost everything they had in the War Between the States. She never knew the luxury of being wealthy but she did know how to move one foot in front of the other and keep going, and she knew how to work. She was a forward-looking woman and when she married my grandfather, an ambitious young salesman, or drummer, as they were called, they made a good team. They founded Dunsmores Dry

Goods Store back when Perryville had dirt streets. They had one daughter, my mother, and I'm sure glad they did." A ripple of laughter went through the crowd. He continued, "She was the one responsible for changing the store into what it is now. She had a vision of times to come and went with the flow. She had the ideas and Grandfather had the force to make it work.

I know that many of you were the recipients of her generosity at one time or another. Maybe it was a little girl going to school barefoot in cold weather because her parents didn't have money for shoes. Or maybe it was a family down on their luck that found a basket of groceries on their doorstep on Thanksgiving Day. Or maybe it was an old lady whose husband was dying and Grandmother thought she shouldn't have to be alone.

That is what all of you see. Now I will tell you what a small boy saw. She was always elegant, with every hair in place and totally 'unflappable'. Nothing I ever did made her love me less. She always had cookies in the cookie jar. If it was empty, she was in the process of making some. Staying the night at Grandmother's house was an event. She had a stereopticon. This was a device that you held up to your eyes and slipped a card into the wire frame about 6 inches in front of your eyes. The pictures were actually two pictures side by side just a little different, and when you looked through the viewer, the subject of the picture jumped right out at you. It came with a basket of pictures of foreign lands, strange animals, and many things a little boy would never have seen. She made me believe that I could be anything I wanted to be, even if I always wanted to be a farmer."

There was a long pause, and Emily wondered if he had forgotten what he wanted to say. Then he said simply, "Good-bye, Grandmother." He left the pulpit and sat down beside Emily again.

When they were in bed that night, Emily said, "I've been with you 15 years, Donald, I don't know if I will ever figure you out entirely."

He answered, "Well, Em, I figured you out when I saw you sitting on my back porch 15 years ago."

"What exactly did you figure out, Mr. Smarty?" she queried, "And how come somebody didn't pick you up before I got here? Did you have some kind of a serious flaw?"

"Maybe it was because I could run faster and I didn't want to get picked up. Maybe I was just waiting for a girl I knew I could love. And when I saw you sitting on my back porch I knew I wanted to get picked up."

Chapter 38

BLOOPER COMES HOME

Until now, trips into town had been reserved for Saturday night. Everybody had a list of supplies to buy, but mostly it was a social evening. All the parking was up and down Main Street and after business was taken care of, the 'big business', which was socializing with neighbors, started. Some would amble up and down Main Street watching for someone to talk with. Others would sit in their cars and wait for someone to walk past whom they could call to. A common sight was to see a man and woman in the front seat with a back seat full of kids, and another family with someone standing at each window talking with their counterparts. Still others gathered on the courthouse lawn. Some of the returning veterans felt free to use the coffee shop, but most of the older ones were still of a Depression mindset and were loath to pay good money for something they had at home.

Vernie and the girls always looked forward to an ice cream cone, if they had been real good. Since they usually were real good about chores and behavior, Emily always tried to squeeze money out of the groceries for a treat. The Magnolia Ice Cream Store on a side street made their own ice cream, had 13 different flavors, and gave huge scoops for a nickel. Sometimes Donald would even pop for one for Emily and himself.

This particular Tuesday an emergency had come up and Donald needed something from the hardware store. The first thing he saw when he entered the store was a couple of strangers looking at the nuts and bolts. He went on about his business but when he went to the counter to pay, they were there discussing something with Buzz Compton, and he had to wait. Buzz went into the backroom and Smiley-face turned to him and said, "We're John and Rex Whiting and we're going to be in town for a while. We are exploring old quarries. They are usually quite deep and spring-fed and you'd be surprised what we find in them."

Dag said, "There's always stories about machines and equipment, even dead bodies in old quarries but there's never been any way to retrieve them. How do you explore these quarries?"

Rex spoke up now, " Ken Berryman out south of town has given us permission to dive into his. He suspects that there may be more than meets the eye in there."

"Dive?" asked Dag. He knew what diving was. You stood on a springboard at the edge of the water and jumped up and down a couple of times, then put your head and hands down and skimmed right into the water as slick as you please.

Rex came back with, " We were in the navy and learned about SCUBA diving. SCUBA stands for 'Self Contained Underwater Breathing Apparatus'. The apparatus is a tank of compressed gas that you wear in a harness on your back. It has a mouthpiece attached so you can stay for long periods underwater. Then you put these rubber fins on your feet and when you paddle it makes you move. It's quite an experience."

Donald had paid for his purchases and the two men started for home. They were almost home when Dag said, "I never heard of this Scooby diving before. It sounds right interesting but I don't know as I want to do it." Donald laughed and then there was more silence. Then Dag wondered, "Do you suppose them fellers will find that old Buick that Clay Dixon brought Molly and Ethel Grace to us in?"

Donald answered, "I don't know. You mentioned that at the time but Pops said not to say anything about it, as he didn't want us to be connected with anything that Clay did. He admitted that he was wanted for bank robbery."

Another short silence and Donald added, "I don't see how they could connect us with anything he did. Nobody came looking for the girls or even questioned where they came from. Em let it be known that they were relatives from Ohio who needed a home."

"Well" Dag said, "It should be interesting anyway."

Emily and Claudia had grown quite close by now. They shared the women's work on the farm and they shared the undertaking of rearing little Joey. Claudia enjoyed her input with the girls, helping them study and teaching them homemaking. They had held several conversations about Claudia finding another partner. Claudia gave all the standard objections like: There are fewer men now. The good ones are all taken. I can't just forget Joey. And Emily had her own list of objections to Claudia staying single: Joey needs to have a father. You need a husband. You don't want to live with us the rest of your life. You need a home of your own to run. Joey needs brothers and sisters. There are a lot of good men out there, but you have to get out and look for them.

September 1947: It was Thursday morning, and the two women were cleaning up the kitchen when Emily looked out the window and saw a shiny new car turn in the drive. Donald had been talking about a new car and she thought,

"Oh, no! He hasn't!" As it turned out, he hadn't. When the occupant of the car opened the door she could see it was Blooper- oops- Frank Adams.

There had been letters from him on a more or less regular basis, but they hadn't seen him since he came home with Joey after Basic Training. He was dressed in civilian clothes, and he seemed a bit more polished. His mouth still had the same twist when he talked and the tic in his eye, maybe caused from nervousness was still prevalent. Joey had told them that he didn't have a very good childhood and he had just sort of fallen in Joey's lap on the bus that took them from the recruiting office. Joey thought Blooper needed a friend and he had proved to be an invaluable friend to Joey. Emily knew why he was here. He had some of Joey's possessions to give to them and he also had some things to tell them about Joey's death. What she didn't know was that Blooper wanted them to be his family almost desperately. Molly had been the one to write to him most faithfully. She was beautiful in his eyes with her red curly hair, blue eyes, and sunny disposition. But she was, after all, only 13 years old to his 23- a mere child. He knew that he could never take Joey's place, but maybe he could make a place of his own.

Emily met him at the door and promptly took his hand and cupped it in both of hers: "I'm so glad to see you, Bloop- do you want to be called Frank? Molly says it is necessary for your dignity," and she gave a small smile. He replied, "Yes, my dad always said I couldn't do anything right so he started calling me Blooper, and the people around Whoopin Holler picked it up. I would really like to change my image. I thought I was going to get rid of that name in the army but there were a couple of fellows who knew me in school that enlisted the same time I did, so the name came right along with me." By this time, Frank was sitting at the kitchen table with a cup of coffee.

Emily had been thinking ahead and now said, "How long can you stay, Frank?" to which he replied, "As long as it takes." She said, "If you can stay all night it would be nice. Then you can tell all of us at once about Joey." Much to his pleasure, they agreed on this plan.

Vernie and the girls stepped down from the school bus at 3:30 and Frank was standing in the parlor window watching. His surprise was matched only by his interest. The girls were both as tall as him, which meant they were about 5'9". They were more striking than he remembered and-yes- polished. They were fast becoming women.

After supper that night, everybody was in the parlor waiting to hear what he had to say about Joey. He reached into a leather folder he carried with him and brought out a V-Mail to Emily: "Maybe I should have mailed this to you right away but I didn't know what was in it and I really thought I should give it to you in person. He had some French money but I couldn't see where it would do you as much good as it did me, so I kept it. I was going to cut the stripes off his jacket but I wanted the authorities to be able to identify him properly. The same way with his Medic armband, but I saved mine to give to you. It was the same as his was." He had turned real sober now: "It was supposed to protect us from the enemy, but there isn't a whole lot of honor on the battlefield." He went on to tell them about his childhood: "My mother died when I was 10 years old. My father was a drunk and he frequently beat my mother and me. I wasn't a big kid and one night when I was 16 years old, I had done something to displease him. He was going to whip me. I knew I couldn't take another beating from him so I grabbed the whip from him and started using it on him. I'm not proud of myself for that, but I would have been less proud to take any more beatings. I ran away that night and walked down to Perryville to the recruiting office. That is when I met Joey, and he gave me the first bit of self-esteem I ever had." He was still for a moment and then: "I have to tell you all this, I wanted so desperately for you to be my family, too. Joey knew this and I think he laid it on a little thick to help me. He said he would always be my friend, no matter what. That part is true, even if he is not with us any more."

Molly spoke out then, "Do you still have the lucky stone that I gave you, Frank?" Frank reached in his pocket and pulled out the stone she had given him. "I carried it clear through the war with me. It must have been a good one. Joey lost his in the landing at Normandy." In the meantime, Ethel Grace was giving Frank the eye, but then decided that he wasn't her type, not that she even knew what her type was. He wasn't very handsome, but maybe that didn't make any difference. Ruthie's Gunter had a big scar across his left cheek but he was still pretty nice. Anyway, she thought that Molly had first dibs on him because of all the letters she had written to him when he was overseas.

"Can you stay a few days, Frank, or are you anxious to get home?" This came from Donald. Frank hesitated a moment and then said, "I'm not going home. I don't have a home any more. I wrote to my dad from Basic Training Camp and never heard anything from him through the whole time I was overseas."

Dag said, "Well, Frank, I think you'd be more than welcome here anytime you want to be here." He looked all around the parlor at each face, and a riot of clapping and hooting broke out accompanied by Donald's slight nod and Emily's kiss that she planted squarely on his cheek.

"Thank you all, I'd be proud to consider myself part of your family. Now I'll tell you what my plans are. I liked being a Medic. I had never given any thought before as to what I wanted to do with my life. So I am going to take advantage of the GI Bill and study medicine. I am already enrolled in UCLA in California." Another round of clapping and hooting and Emily said, "I would really hope that someday you would go back to Whoopin Holler and attempt to make peace with your father." Frank shrugged his shoulders and the talk turned to generalities. Soon the party broke up. Frank was shown to Joey's old room and there was a chorus of 'Good-nights' as they all retired.

Frank was due to report to UCLA in 2 weeks so he stayed for another 5 days. Monday morning, he and Donald went into town to get chicken feed for Emily's flock. Frank decided that he needed some new clothes but wanted mostly to wait until he got to California to see what the other students were wearing. When they came home, they were full of talk they had heard in town. John and Rex Whiting had been diving into the old quarry and guess what they had found! The quarry was about 400 feet deep and in the bottom of it there was an old lawn mower, a rowboat, a lobster trap (?), and an old tan Buick. A knowing look passed between Dag and Donald, and Emily asked, "What are they going to do now?" Donald said, "Talk is that they are going to haul the car out and try to see who it belonged to."

That night in the bedroom, Emily said, "Do you think that old car is the one Clay Dixon drove here?" "I do," said Donald "But I don't think they will ever connect it to us. Word is that the FBI will get into it if they can identify it. They may be able to connect it with some crimes back then. The thing is that Berryman saw someone dump it in the quarry and has the exact date it happened."

Emily said, "I saw Clay when he drove in that day. He didn't even slow down until he was around behind the barn out of sight. I knew right then that he didn't want to be seen. My worry is that they might be able to connect it to the girls. I am hoping that they will not even remember the car."

Donald said, "If the Feds come here asking questions we will have to tell them the truth, which means that the girls will have to know the truth. I think they are pretty strong girls and we have tried to give them a peg to hang their hats on, so, Em, I think we will make it through whatever happens. We'll just keep our heads low in the water and hope they don't notice us."

Chapter 39

Old Friends - 1950

Vern and Dag had become friends after Dag's wife ran off with the drummer fellow and his little girl back in 1904. Never mind that she was Vern's sister. He did not approve of her actions and felt a great compassion toward Dag, Their friendship had grown over the years and they could aptly be called 'best buddies'. Vern held out hopes that he would move back to the farm when the 'younguns' were gone but for now he spent every Sunday at the farm. He and Dag were both 69 years old now and not too much disposed to physical labor so they just sort of lazed around, went fishing, went to auction sales now and then, made things out in the woodshop and did light chores to help Donald and Vernie. There was one thing they had always talked about but never got around to doing. They wanted to fish the Pemberton River up in Virginia for Rainbow Trout.

Dag said, "Maybe it's now or never. You still got all our old camping stuff?" Vern said, "Sure have, but it's all old. Must have been 25 years since we went camping." So the two of them went to the attic and brought down the tent, sleeping bags that Flora had made for them, the cookware, and all the other accumulation of past outings.

The trip was planned for the second week in July. Emily and Claudia cooked up a storm so they could send food with them. On a Sunday morning with all their equipment in the old pickup truck they left with big grins on their faces. It was a hundred miles away, which is probably why they hadn't actually done it before. They planned on being back in 4 days, "Because," Vern said, "we're not sure if our old bones can handle sleepin' on the ground any more."

On Monday they caught a mess of trout and cooked them over an open campfire. On Tuesday they did the same thing. On Wednesday, Vern looked up at the sky and said, "I don't know! It feels like rain. Maybe we should just pack up and go home." Dag said, "We'll do whatever you want to but I sure would like to get another mess of trout to take home. We could stop in town and get a bucket of ice and be home in 3 hours. We could fish for a couple of hours and still leave here by noon." Vern agreed that it sounded like a plan and they took their fishing gear upstream in the river and started fishing.

Vern was keeping a concerned eye on the sky as it looked like it was raining up in the mountains. At 10 o'clock there was a booming sound like thunder and a wall of water 12 feet high came around the bend in the river. Vern shouted, "FLASH FLOOD! GET OUT OF THE WATER!" But Dag was out a bit farther and Vern started toward him to help him get out. He saw the wall of water take his old friend and toss him in the air. Seconds later, Vern himself was caught by the rushing waves and they both went down the river.

Thursday morning at breakfast, Donald said, " Today is the day the great fishermen will return." Emily and Claudia smiled. Claudia and little Joey were being sparked by Evan Jordan, the owner of the Western Auto Store in town, and she smiled a whole lot more than she used to. Emily thought it was a good thing to see. She said, "What time do you think they will be back, Donald?" He replied, "I expect they'll be coming in around 4 o'clock."

By six o'clock when they still hadn't returned, the folks at home were getting worried about them. Donald called the Sheriff and asked if he could find out if there had been any accidents. He said he could and he would. He called Colonel Alger of the State Police who said there had been no accidents. When Colonel Alger called the State Police of Virginia, the dispatcher said there were no accidents but there had been a flashflood up on the Pemberton River this morning and he thought there might be quite a number of casualties. Donald's heart fell into his boots. He knew as sure as anything on this earth what had happened to his father and father-in-law.

News Bulletin, July 20, 1976

Pembroke, Virginia: Beginning about 7:00 AM last Friday morning a thunderstorm towering over 50,000 feet stalled near Hague's Peak in the upper reaches of the Big Thomas Canyon.

The torrential downpour from that storm put almost 12 inches of rainfall in the Glen Comfort and Pembroke areas in just four hours. This normally pleasant river rapidly became a raging torrent as the volume of water reached a peak 31,000 cfs, far above the 200 cfs that normally flow through the narrows.

The resulting flash flood caused destruction as far as the Runnymede River southeast of Winona Falls, Virginia. It destroyed homes, businesses, and roads...

It took the lives of 144 people.

He went home and told the family what he had found out. Emily was stunned. So were the rest of them, for that matter. He said, "Em, you and I will leave here in 40 minutes and drive up there. We should get there by midnight. Get some things put together for us to stay overnight- maybe a couple of nights." She went into the bedroom and the girls and Claudia followed her. They all knew how flash floods worked. "Will you girls be all right here? Vernie will be with you." They assured her they would be but asked her to call home if she found out anything.

Forty minutes later, she and Donald were getting in the car when the back door opened and Vernie came running out with some things hastily thrown into a pillowcase. He announced, "I'm going with you. They're my grandpas. I can help you." Donald had a feeling that it wouldn't do any good to argue so he said, "Get in." and he ran to the house and told Claudia that Vernie would be going with them. She nodded her agreement.

They arrived at Pembroke a little after midnight and went straight to the Sheriff's office. When Donald had told them his story, one of the men said, "We could see where somebody had a camp up on the Pemberton, but nobody is there now. There is an old green pickup truck and the remains of a camp back away from the water enough to keep them intact." Emily was crying and Vernie was trying to comfort her. There isn't anything we can do tonight but we'll start searching at dawn tomorrow. Do you have anyone to stay with tonight?" When Donald told him they didn't, he said, "I imagine that all the lodging places are full. I'll see if my Aunt Nora will put you up tonight." After a telephone conversation with Aunt Nora, he said, "Come along, she's got room for you."

At 6 o'clock on Friday morning, Emily, Vernie, and Donald stood on the edge of the now calm river scanning the opposite shore. A reporter came up behind them and took a picture of them standing side by side, which would live in mortality for 50 years. Emily said, "What are you thinking, Donald?" and he answered, "I think they are gone. We will be lucky if they even find any bodies. Emily started crying; Donald and Vernie were desperately trying to keep the tears at bay. "What are we going to do, Dad?" Vernie asked. "Nothing we can do except wait to see if anybody finds them. I guess what we could do is to pack up all of their gear and get ready to take it home." All three of them started picking up gear and cleaning up the campsite. Donald drove the truck and Emily and Vernie followed in the car. She was glad Vernie had come along with them. She would call Claudia when they got back to Pembroke and tell her what was happening.

They had been staying at Aunt Nora's boarding house for three days when they decided it was time to go home. No sign had been found of the two old men and the sheriff said the bodies could turn up later miles from where they disappeared. It was a sad entourage that headed out for Perryville that morning. Emily wished badly that she was riding with Donald, but the anguish would be worse if Vernie was driving the car by himself. Besides, she knew that Vernie had feelings about his grandfathers and didn't deserve to be left alone to thrash them out.

When they arrived at the house, Garr and Bear met them in the drive. Emily had asked Claudia to call them, knowing that they would be on their way in minimum time. She had also apprised Ruthie of the events that were happening. The two old men had obviously been crying. They had gone into town to the Cemetery Office to see about buying a plot so as to have a place to bury Dag if the occasion arose. Everybody felt by now that the occasion would arise. To their surprise and joy the plot next to Dunsmore's was for sale by an individual. There was room for four and since they had never given it a thought until now, felt very fortunate to have acquired the plot right next to their second family.

When a week had passed and nothing had been found, they all decided to try and get on with their lives. The Uncles went home and life continued as usual for the family. Everybody was sad and they could hardly mention Dag and Vern without breaking into tears.

August 10, 1950

Dear Frank,

I have some very sad news to tell you. Grandpa Dag and Pops went fishing up on the Pemberton River at Pembroke, Virginia. It had been a 30-year dream of theirs and they decided to make it come true while they still could. They were camping up there on the 12th of July when the flash flood that took 144 lives came down the Pemberton washing everything in it's way down the river. Mom and Dad went up there and packed up the camp, which was on higher ground and brought everything home. There was no sign of our two men. The sheriff up there told Dad that it might be weeks before the bodies show up and maybe they never will. I will keep you informed as to any further events. If you write back send it to Mom and Dad, as they are heartbroken.

As always, Your Friend, Molly Morrison

August 21, 1950

Dear Family,

Molly has written to me the horrible news about the Grandpas. I am stunned. It seems to me that they should have gone on forever. I wish I could hop on an airplane and be there in a few hours, but- maybe I will.

I am on break from school right now and don't need to be back until September 1.

Your son, Frank Adams

He prepared the letter for mailing knowing that he might be there before the letter was. Then he scurried around doing the things he had to do to get ready and in two hours he was on his way.

Molly stood at the cosmetic counter at the store. No customers were in sight and she was brooding. Suddenly she heard a familiar voice. It was saying, "Good Golly, Miss Molly! You are prettier than I have ever seen you. You just keep on improving all the time. Oh, not that there was so much room for improvement" Then he stopped for a moment, and continued, "I'm babbling!"

Molly said, "FRANK! I didn't know you were coming."

"Nobody did," he said, "the letter telling them about my visit will probably get here tomorrow." On impulse, and entirely unplanned, he said, "I decided to start looking for a wife, and who is the first one I see when I hit town? Miss Molly, of course." All Molly could do was stare. He continued, "Oh, not right away, but it's something to think about."

"Is this a proposal, Frank?" she asked.

"No," he said, "But it will be some day. The first time I saw you the morning that Joey and I went into the Army I thought you were the prettiest little thing I had ever seen. At that time I didn't feel like any girl would ever want me- old Blooper, who couldn't do anything right. Well, things have changed. I am almost ready to graduate and become a veterinarian. I have something to offer now."

She said, "I don't think we should mention this to the folks as they would say I am too young to even be engaged."

"You are, and that's why I'm not proposing now. You need to know that is what I am going to do when the time is right."

Every weekend the Uncles drove the Packard 8 over to Perryville to get the latest report on finding Dag and Vern. It was the first week in September and the holidays had been a bittersweet affair The Uncles had not left for home yet, in fact, Donald was beginning to wonder if they wanted to settle in and live with them. Not that they weren't welcome but, in reality, Donald had given some thought as to when he and Emily would have an empty nest. Just when he decided he could stand to have them around some more in light of the fact that they were getting old, they announced that they were going home.

Right after breakfast, the telephone rang with their party line ring. Donald picked it up and then his face went white and he just stood there like a stone. It was the sheriff at Pembroke saying that two bodies had been found at Winona Falls, about 20 miles from the campsite. He said the description fit but they needed somebody to identify them. He looked on the map to see how to get to Winona Falls. He urged Emily to stay at home saying he didn't know what kind of shape they were in. Uncle Bear said, "You stay here, Emmy-girl, and Garr and me will go with Donald. She agreed and in less than an hour the threesome was on its way.

Winona Falls was a fair sized town and the local undertaker had the two bodies in his cold vault in the basement. He warned the men that they had deteriorated some but not beyond recognition, so they were more or less prepared for what they were to see. However, assumption and reality are two different things, and the minute he pulled the sheets back, Garr began to sob uncontrollably. Bear was busy trying to take care of Garr, and Donald wanted to sob himself.

The undertaker made quick work of it and asked Donald to come into his office. He called Simon Beck at Perryville and told him about the bodies, said they had been identified and that Donald was right here with him. He talked to Donald and agreed to come to Winona Falls and pick them up. He said he would call Donald when he got back home.

"Just one more thing," Donald said to the sheriff, " I want to see where they were found. These men are my father and my wife's father and I know she is going to want to see it, too. Is it accessible from the road?" The sheriff hesitated, and then said, "There would be a little walking. Why don't you wait until emotions have cooled a bit then come back and I will give you a personal tour? Or better yet, Deputy Richards here will give you a personal tour. It is on his father's farm. Donald shook hands with the deputy and took his phone number and said he would call him when they were ready.

Vernie had been acting a bit strange- maybe secretive was the word. Donald had seen a light on in the old tack room in the barn late last night. Now he was looking around in there to see what somebody had been doing. He was pretty sure it involved Vernie. The old horse blanket that should have been on the shelf was over in the corner. When he picked it up, there was the frame he had made for Old Prancer's hat, but it was empty. Nothing else was out of place that he could see. Shaking his head, he went into the house for breakfast.

They were almost finished eating when Vernie cleared his throat and said, "Dad, I need some things from the drug store. Can I take the truck for a while?" Donald was fairly sure that he didn't need anything from the drug store, and since he wasn't quite 16, he didn't have a driver's license yet. He had actually been driving for a couple of years now but mostly on the farm and in the country. Doing some fast reckoning, Donald said, "I have some things to get in town, why don't we go in together." Vernie quickly wiped the disappointed look off his face and said, "That'll be all right. Can I drive?"

He came out of the house carrying a brown paper bag a few minutes later and put it behind the seat in the truck. In town, Donald said "Why don't I leave you at the drug store and go on down to the feed store? You can come down there when you're ready." Vernie agreed, as the place he really wanted to go was over on the next street. He got out and reached in back and grabbed the paper sack. Donald watched him walk away with a puzzled look. A horn tooted behind him, and he thought, "Oh well, he's a good kid, maybe he'll talk about it on the way home."

Simon Beck in his office at the Funeral Home saw the kid come out of the alley down the street behind the drugstore. "Isn't that the Morrison Kid?" he asked himself. "He seems to be coming this way. I wonder what he's up to?" To Simon's surprise, the kid came up the walk and opened the front door. He had on blue jeans and was carrying a paper bag. He said, "Mr. Beck, I'm Vernie Morrison, and I want to ask a favor of you."

"I won't open the caskets if that's what you want." Simon said.

"No, that's not what I want," Vernie said as he pulled a disreputable old straw hat with holes in the side out of the paper bag. "I want you to put this in the casket with my Grandpa Dag. It was his old mules hat. He loved that old mule and when I was born he gave it to me as a present. My dad made a frame and hung it on the wall in my room."

Now Simon was truly perplexed. An old straw hat for a baby present? Not just any straw hat but one that belonged to a mule. He had always thought that Dag was a little strange. Maybe it was one of those recessive genes the scientists talked about that was going down through a family. Now he could see how much this meant to the boy, and he gathered all of his undertaker composure about him and said, "I will certainly do that, son. Could I say that you want this to be a secret?" Vernie nodded his head slightly, thanked Simon, and went out the front door.

Vernie didn't have much to say on the way home, but he seemed pleased with himself, the paper bag was missing, and he no longer acted so secretive. Donald had somewhat of an idea about what had been transpiring by now. He decided to just keep his mouth shut unless Vernie wanted to talk about it.

On September 12, 1950, Vern was laid to rest in his plot beside Flora, and Dag was laid to rest 12 feet away in his brothers' plot. There were 300 people attending. The casket was closed and the brothers had themselves under control. This time it was Emily who wanted to do the eulogy, but Donald also wanted to say a few words about Pops, so they both went forward. Emily spoke first and told about how much both men had meant to her. Then it was Donald's turn, and his message was a somewhat simple one: "The Gods of the River were angry the day they stirred the river up into a flash flood. They said, "These two men have been together for 50 years. They need to stay together for eternity." They took these two together, carried them 20 miles downriver and deposited them in the same little cove in a peaceful farm setting." I think we can take some measure of comfort in this."

The ladies of the church put on a dinner after the burial and there was even some laughter as the townspeople exchanged stories about the two men.

That night at home, Vernie, who was now 15 years old, turned to the family before he went upstairs, and said, " Now that Grandpa Vern is gone, I want to be called 'Vern'. I am getting too old to be called Vernie any more." Before anyone could laugh and hurt his dignity, Donald said, "I agree with you, and Pops would be the first one to say he was proud that you want to be called 'Vern'. So, listen up, all you gathered here for this important meeting, meet Mr. Vern Morrison, not to be mistaken for Pops. They all responded with "Hi, Vern," and "Pleased to meetcha, Vern." Ruthie said, "Vern! Vern! Lean and tight! Drives that car with all his might!"

Chapter 40

MOLLY AND UNCLE BEAR

Frank returned for the funeral and he and Molly announced their engagement. Emily and Donald were not real pleased. They thought she was much too young and said so. Frank countered with, "We'll not be getting married until Molly is out of school and feels like it is time. I have loved her since the day I saw her at the recruiting office telling Joey good-bye. Now I have my degree in veterinary medicine so I will be able to take care of a family. Maybe you had hoped for a handsome dude for such a pretty daughter, but I try to make myself handsome inside, and I keep telling myself that is what counts." At this declaration of love, the Morrisons caved in, and agreed to the engagement.

Secretly the couple made plans to be married the next June. The next April, Garrett developed a cough that wouldn't go away. He went to the doctor and was taking the newfound miracle drugs, but the cough just seemed to get deeper and tighter. It went from bronchitis into pneumonia, and within 2 weeks, he had passed away. His death affected no one more than it did Bear. The funeral was held in Perryville and, afterward, Bear did not seem to make any move to go home. He told Molly, who had always been a favorite, through a watershed of tears that he had never been separated from his twin one night in his life, except, of course, the time he had appendicitis and was in the hospital for a week. He didn't honestly know how he was going back to live in their house without Garr. When Donald approached him about this and heard his story, he said, "Why don't you go home and get some clothes, take care of whatever you have to, and come back until you feel better about going home? You can have Dag's room for as long as you need it." Accompanied by Molly, he set out the next day to do just that.

Molly had always been interested in the Sears, Roebuck house that the uncles had built in 1936 near Gulchy Gap, and now she made a production of checking everything out preparatory to leaving it empty for a while. Thoughtfully, Bear helped her clean out the refrigerator, turn off the water, and drain the water pipes just like Donald had told them to. Finally he said, "You and Frank got a place to live yet?" She assured him that they had not had time to look. "He could probably have a pretty healthy business in town here. We haven't ever had a Vet and Gulchy Gap is already busting at the seams." Molly did not see at first what he was getting at, and then she said, "I would have to ask him." Bear started weeping profusely, and meekly told her, "Truth is, Miss Molly, that I'm scared to live alone. Garr and me- we always took care of each other, just like I took care of him when he got sick. Neither one of us ever gave a thought to one of us goin' and leavin' the other. If you and Frank would move in with me, I promise I wouldn't be hardly any trouble. I keep myself and my home clean and neat. You don't hardly ever see a speck of dust on anything. I know how to clean house, do gardening, and I can even cook" She laughed, "You sound like you're applying for a job as a servant." "I'm just wantin' to carry my share of the load," he said.

Molly was driving the Packard 8 and she drove about 5 miles in silence before she said, "Uncle Bear, we'll just keep this conversation to ourselves while I talk things over with Frank. For now, everything will be all right. Dad even told me that he would bring the horses over to the farm so you could take care of them." For the first time since his brother had died, Bear had a smile on his lips.

May 1, 1951

Dearest Frank,

I have something exciting to tell you. Uncle Bear wants us to come and live with him. He says he is scared to live alone without Uncle Garr. They have never been apart before and he doesn't want to go home without someone else there. He also says that you should be able to run a good business from the barn and Grandpa Dag's log house. What do you think? Have you ever been to Gulchy Gap? I have never lived with him but he is going to be staying at our house for a while so I should be able to know if we could live with him. I have always liked the Uncles. Mama says I am not going down to the courthouse to get married. She says we can have a small wedding right at home. I would like that.

All my Love, Molly

May 15, 1951

Miss Molly My Love,

Your plan sounds like something to look into. I don't know Uncle Bear
well enough to say yes or no. It would save us a pretty penny to not have
to buy furniture or pay rent for a while. It gives me kind of a pleasure
to think of turning the barn and the log house into a business. I think I
would want to go there and stay a few days to get a feel for the town and
the people. I will be home the first of June. If we are going to get
married the 28th that will give me time to spend a few days in Gulchy
Gap. I can hardly imagine living in a town called Gulchy Gap,
especially when I came from Blossom Falls and Whoopin Holler.
Maybe you could persuade Uncle Bear to go with me and show me
around.

All my love, Frank

When Frank came home, Bear was ready to go. They were going to take the
Packard 8, as Frank didn't have a car as yet. In three days they came back and
both of them were bubbling over with excitement. Bear had taken him all up
and down Main St. and introduced him to all the merchants. They had
thoroughly inspected the buildings Frank was interested in and found them
agreeable to his plans. Part of Bear's excitement was that he would be living in
his own house again. Not that living with the Morrisons was bad, but he said
that 'home was where your stuff was'.

By the middle of August, Bear, Frank, and Molly were settled into the Sears
Roebuck house, remodeling was going forward on the barn, and Frank and
Molly had bought a used car. Molly didn't even notice the way that Frank had
a funny little twist to his lips when he talked.

Chapter 41

ANNIVERSARY OF OMAHA BEACH

For six years Molly, Frank, and Uncle Bear lived happily in the Sears Roebuck house. The old man was 81 years old and one morning in 1957, Molly was not surprised to find him in his bed sleeping peacefully forever. She was more surprised to find that Bear had left all his worldly possessions to her. This included the 1936 Packard 8 Phaeton, which had been on blocks out in the shed since Garr had died. Frank had kept the old car in mint condition and it was up on blocks in the shed most of the time. It came out of hiding once a year to be driven in the 4th of July parade. This meant that she and Frank had truly been given a head start.

Molly had wanted children but they just didn't seem to be in the plan, so she had turned all her attention on Frank and Bear. Frank was a little more disappointed as he had been an only child with a somewhat inadequate childhood, but his business was moving right along and he had built kennels for dogs and cages for cats in his facility. There was a box stall out in the barn for the occasional horse that needed treatment. He was doing a fairly brisk business with farm animals, but, of course, he had to do house calls (or barn calls) for large animals like cows and pigs. The log house had been renovated for an office and examination rooms, and Molly worked as the receptionist. It was a good working arrangement.

Then 9 years after they were married a miracle occurred. In 1960, Molly found herself with child. Frank was so ecstatic; he went out and bought a new pickup truck. He also bought the front porch swing that Molly had wanted and took her out to dinner. In September a little girl was born and they named her Nancy after Molly's mother. Frank, who had wanted a son, sighed and said, "Oh, well! Maybe the next one will be a boy." They were to wait 10 more years before the little boy whom they named Barrett materialized.

In 1969 the 25th anniversary of the Battle of Normandy would be noted on the news and some television shows. It wouldn't be until the 50th that a reunion of old Army buddies was considered, but Frank had been doing a lot of thinking about it. Emily was 67 and Donald was 68, and somewhere in the back of his mind, Frank had wanted to take them to see Joey's grave for a long time. One Sunday at dinner, he said, "Dad, how about you and Mom take a trip to France with Molly and me?"

Donald said, "Now why would we want to do that. I've always wanted to go to Yellowstone."

Emily spoke quietly, "I think he wants to show us where Joey died and where he is buried, Donald." A stricken look appeared on Donald's face. How could he have forgotten? That had always been Emily's one great wish, and how could he equate that with Yellowstone, a place that would always be a possibility. He couldn't even bring forth words to say how he felt. Finally he stammered, " I'm sorry, Em, of course you are right. If I never see Yellowstone it will not be a great big loss, but not seeing where Joey is would be."

He looked at Frank and said, "How much would this cost us?" As with others of his generation, cost would always be first and foremost. Frank now stated, "We have been blessed by the Uncles who gave us a big boost in our life's goals. I was blessed by having Joey take me under his wing in the Army. I was blessed by you folks for taking me into your family, and I was blessed by Miss Molly for marrying me and giving me a daughter. We will pay the costs if you will go with us. We would like to be there on June 6 as there will be celebrations then, and I might even see some of my old Army mates." It took Emily and Donald about 30 minutes to decide that they could go.

Vern was married with two small sons and he and his family lived in the big farmhouse and worked the farm. The rural kids were going into town on the school bus now and Donald had purchased the old schoolhouse a mile down and remodeled it into a home for him and Emily. Sunday dinners were now held at someone else's house. He still helped Vern with the farm work when he wanted to, but mostly he kept the machinery in repair. Vern had wanted nothing to do with the store so that had mostly reverted to Ruthie's responsibility. She had made a good thing of the Bridal Shoppe and Gunter handled the Menswear well. Claudia had finally accepted Evan Jordan's pursuit and she was now Mrs. Western Auto of Perryville.

Ethel Grace had decided that she wanted to continue her education and was now a high school math teacher with three small sons married to a CPA or Certified Public Accountant in Perryville. So there wasn't anyone who was going to suffer a great deal if the older couple was gone for a few weeks.

On May 28th, the two couples and Nancy flew to Fairoaks Airfield at Surrey, England. There they boarded a twin-engined aircraft, and flew over Portsmouth Harbour before crossing the Channel. During the hour's flight the guide, with the help of charts, briefed them on the strategic situation in Europe during the months leading up to D-Day - naval, air, military strengths on both western and eastern fronts; Hitler's command style against Churchill and Roosevelt's and the tactical dilemmas facing both sides.

Landing at Cherbourg Airport in France they met the driver and started an overland tour of the Normandy D-Day Beaches. First they visited Omaha Beach, still referred to by its wartime name, a peaceful four-mile stretch of sand, which belies the ferocity of the fighting that befell it on June 6th 1944. They walked on Omaha Beach and after thoughtfully looking over the layout of the beach; Frank started walking to the left. When he reached a certain point, he said, "I can't be real sure but I think this right here is where we were the day Joey died. His voice faltered and he fought for control. Emily was the one he thought might be upset, but for just a moment he was back in 1944, and was standing over Joey who had a big red spot on his chest. Emily reached over and touched his shoulder, and the feeling of terror left him. He continued, "It was the second or third day. I can't remember which, and we were getting ready to move forward and find our company. There was a German bunker right up there," and he pointed, then said, "By Golly, Miss Molly, it's still there!" She could see what looked like a rough spot in the side of a hill. Frank said then, "I can almost shut my eyes and be back here on D-Day with all the gunfire, screams, landing craft sinking, dying men-" Molly said, "Stop it, Frank. You aren't doing yourself any good by remembering all this." "I know. I didn't intend to get off on this track. It just came out of the blue."

The Normandy American Cemetery at St Laurent where almost 10,000 Americans lie buried and over 1,500 missing Americans are commemorated, was next, and the Pointe du Hoc cliffs scaled by 2 US Rangers on D- Day. The cliff heights are still deeply pitted with German bunkers and shell holes. They took in stunning views as they flew over the wreck of Mulberry Harbor - an artificial harbor that protected the landings of the vast numbers of men and vehicles during the invasion.

A Mulberry harbor was a type of temporary harbor developed in World War II to offload cargo on the beaches during the Allied invasion of Normandy. The Mulberry harbors were two prefabricated or *artificial* military harbors, which were taken across the English Channel from Britain with the invading army in sections and assembled off the coast of Normandy as part of the D-Day invasion of France. The harbors were made up of all the elements one would expect of any harbor: breakwater, piers, roadways etc.

By June 9, just 3 days after D-Day, two harbors codenamed Mulberry 'A' and 'B' were constructed at Omaha Beach and Arromanches, respectively. However, a large storm on June 19 destroyed the American harbor at Omaha, leaving only the British harbor, which came to be known as Port Winston at Arromanches. While the harbor at Omaha was destroyed sooner than expected (due to it not being securely anchored to the sea bed), Port Winston saw heavy use for 8 months—despite being designed to last only 3 months. In the 100 days after D-Day, it was used to land over 2.5 million men, 500,000 vehicles, and 4 million tons of supplies providing much needed reinforcements in France.

A complete Mulberry harbor was constructed out of 600,000 tons of concrete between 33 jetties, and had 10 miles (15 km) of floating roadways to land men and vehicles on the beach. Port Winston is commonly upheld as one of the best examples of military engineering. Its remains are still visible today from the beaches at Arromanches, and a section of it remains embedded in the sand in the Thames Estuary, accessible at low tide, about 100 m off the coast of the military base at Shoeburyness. A Phoenix unit known as The Far Mulberry sank off Pagham and lying at about 10 metres is an easily accessible scuba diving site.

The Normandy American Cemetery and Memorial in France is located on the site of the temporary American St. Laurent Cemetery, established by the U.S. First Army on June 8, 1944 and the first American cemetery on European soil in World War II. The cemetery site, at the north end of its ½ mile access road, covers 172.5 acres and contains the graves of 9,387 of our military dead, most of whom lost their lives in the D-Day landings and ensuing operations. On the Walls of the Missing in a semicircular garden on the east side of the memorial are inscribed 1,557 names. Rosettes mark the names of those since recovered and identified.

The memorial consists of a semicircular colonnade with a terrace at each end containing large maps and narratives of the military operations; at the center is the bronze statue, "Spirit of American Youth." An orientation table overlooking the beach depicts the landings in Normandy. Facing west at the memorial, one sees in the foreground the reflecting pool; beyond is the burial area with a circular chapel and, at the far end, granite statues representing the U.S. and France.

Frank guided them up to the cemetery office to look at the guidebook and find out where Joey's grave was located. "Ah, here it is. Section 154, site # 82." They boarded the shuttle car to take them to Section 154, then walked until they found site # 82. The white wooden cross had a bronze plaque inscribed with 'Lieutenant Joseph H. Jones, Medic for 29th Infantry Division- 1st Army USA-1923-1944'. They stood there, each engrossed in his own thoughts until they heard a soft sob coming from Frank. Then Emily understood that this trip was as much for him as it was for her. She and Molly stood on each side of him and gently urged him to turn back to the Memorial.

Later, as they were getting ready for bed, he said, "I'm sorry, Molly, I didn't think it was going to affect me that way." She said, "You have nothing to be sorry about, Frank. Honest emotion isn't anything to be ashamed of. And you might have given Mama something to think about to help her keep her chin up."

Chapter 42

LETTER FROM CLAY

November 1970

Mrs. Morrison,

I want to thank you for taking care of my girls. I think you did keep them as I could see you were a caring person. They deserved better than me. I got caught and spent 30 years in prison for the bank robbery. Life has not been easy for me. It has been one mishap after another. I have worked at piddlin' jobs for little pay. I'm not complaining, as I have nobody but myself to blame. I came to Perryville a few years ago to see my daughters, but when I inquired about them, and found out that you and your husband have given them a good start in life, I decided to back off. They didn't need me.

Now for the good part. I have discovered the People's Temple. It was founded by an ordained minister of *The Disciples of Christ* church in Indiana, Jim Jones, in the 1950s. It is an inter-racial mission for the sick, homeless, and jobless. He preaches a 'social gospel' of human freedom, equality, and love, which requires helping the least and lowliest of society's members. Shortly after it was founded, He moved to Ukiah in South California. He believed the end of the world would be caused by nuclear war, and Ukiah is believed to be one of the places in the US that can survive a nuclear attack. This is where I came in. I guess I was looking for something to give meaning to my life, and I found it. I have seen him cure cancer, heart disease, and arthritis.

The Temple has leased almost 4,000 acres of dense jungle from the government of Guyana in South America. We will establish an agricultural cooperative there, and call it the *"Peoples Temple Agricultural Project."* We will raise animals for food, and assorted tropical fruits and vegetables for consumption and sale. Everyone will have a portion of the work to do but they will benefit immensely from the loving care they receive. I can't say enough about how this has affected me. It has changed my life completely. I don't know what you have told the girls about me or if you want to tell them anything, however, I think they must be 35 years now. They are adult enough to know about me. It is your choice. I will not be making an appearance in their lives. I just wanted you to know that I think you have done a marvelous thing for them.

Respectfully, Clay Harrington (Dixon)

Emily presented the letter to Donald and asked him what he thought. The first words out of his mouth were, "Dang it, we took those girls and adopted them and fed them and educated them. Why does he think they are *his* daughters?"

Emily replied, "Well, they do know that we adopted them and they know that their father left them with us. They are 35 years old now and have become who they are going to be. Could it hurt them, or us, for them to know about this?"

After a moment of thought, he said, "No, I guess not. They have always been good girls and have given us a minimum of trouble. You are right, they have a right to see this letter. I just hope they won't feel compelled to bring him back into our lives."

Emily called each of them and invited them for Sunday dinner. After dinner she said, "We had a reason for asking you here today." She and Donald sat down at the dining table and the others followed. She continued, " I received a letter from Clay Dixon. I am not going to say your father because your father is sitting right here with us." The two girls nodded in agreement. Ethel Grace was first to speak up, "I don't mind telling you that I don't much care what he has to say. He went away and left us and we never heard another word." Her husband, Rob, said, "Now, Ethel Grace, don't go getting a twist in your panties. You don't even know what he has to say."

Molly chimed in with, " Does he want something from us, because I'm of the same mind as Ethel Grace is. He's never done anything for us except to abandon us in a providential spot."

Emily replied, "I don't get the feeling that he wants anything from you. Why don't you read it, Molly?" She handed the letter over to Molly, who proceeded to read it out loud. When she was through, they all sat there trying to digest it. The girls had never given him a whole lot of thought. Finally, Ethel

Grace said, "It doesn't change my mind one bit. I do not want a relationship with him. I am not going to answer it."

Donald said, "I think that it would be right nigh impossible to write to him. He didn't even put a return address on the envelope. I think maybe that was a Freudian slip. I don't think he really wants a relationship either."

Molly said, "I feel the same as Ethel Grace. We have a life here and it doesn't include him. He made some choices when we were little that disallowed any room for us in his life. So be it!"

Emily answered, " I understand what you are saying, but we thought you should know about the letter, anyway. He seems to have found some meaning to life and for that, I am glad. We certainly knew that he didn't have a clue about that when he left you girls with us.

Donald seemed to just remember something: "Do you remember when divers went down into Berryman's Stone Quarry and found an old Buick?" Ethel Grace said, "Yes, it was after the war wasn't it?" "Well," Donald said, "We never admitted that we knew anything about it, but that old Buick was the one Clay drove when he brought you here. He admitted to us that he was wanted for a bank robbery and the Buick was stolen. We told him not to leave it here. Grandpa Dag predicted that it would probably wind up in Berryman's Quarry and we made a pact to never say that to anyone because we didn't want to be part of an FBI investigation. Clay had driven it around behind the barn when he came so none of the neighbors ever saw it at our place. No one ever came and asked us about it and we want to keep it that way."

Frank, who had been silent up until now, said, "Statute of Limitations has run out anyway, and Clay has paid for his crime so I doubt anyone will ask us anything."

1978: Mass suicide leaves 900 dead: The bodies of 914 people, including 276 children, have been found in Guyana in South America. Most of the dead - members of the People's Temple Christian Church - had consumed a soft drink laced with cyanide and sedatives.

However, the body of the People's Temple charismatic leader, Jim Jones, was said to have a bullet wound in the right temple, believed to be self-inflicted. The deaths are being linked to the earlier killings of five people, including US Congressman Leo Ryan, on a nearby airstrip.

Mr. Ryan had led a fact-finding mission to the church's jungle settlement - Jonestown - after allegations by relatives in the US of human rights abuses.

Last year Jim Jones and most of the 1,000 members of the People's Temple moved to Guyana from San Francisco after an investigation began into the church for tax evasion.

People who had left the organization told the authorities of brutal beatings, murders and a mass suicide plan but were not believed.

In spite of the tax evasion allegations, Jim Jones was still widely respected for setting up a racially mixed church, which helped the disadvantaged.

The Peoples Temple was initially structured as an inter-racial mission for the sick, homeless and jobless. He assembled a large following of over 900 members in Indianapolis IN during the 1950's.

"He preached a 'social gospel' of human freedom, equality, and love, which required helping the least and the lowliest of society's members. Later on, however, this gospel became explicitly socialistic, or communistic in Jones' own view, and the hypocrisy of white Christianity was ridiculed while 'apostolic socialism' was preached."

It was an interracial congregation — almost unheard of in Indiana at the time. When a government investigation began into his cures for cancer, heart disease and arthritis, he decided to move the group to Ukiah in Northern California. He preached the imminent end of the world in a nuclear war; Esquire magazine listed Ukiah as one of nine in the U.S. that could survive a nuclear attack. They later moved to San Francisco and Los Angeles. After an expose during the mid 1970's in the magazine *New West* raised suspicions of illegal activities within the Temple, he moved some of the Temple membership to Jonestown, Guyana.

Statement of a survivor: "The 'total dedication' you once observed of me was not to Jim Jones – it was to an organization of people who had nothing left to lose. No matter what view one takes of the Temple, perhaps the most relevant truth is that it was filled with outcasts and the poor who were looking for something they could not find in our society. And sadly enough, there are millions more out there with all kinds of different, but desperate needs whose lives will end tragically, as happens every day. No matter how you cut it, you just can't separate Jonestown from America, because the Peoples Temple was not born in a vacuum, and despite the attempt to isolate it, neither did it end in one."

The first headlines claimed that 407 Temple members had been killed and that the remainder had fled into the jungle. This death count was revised several times over the next week until the final total of 914 was reached. This total included 276 children.

Emily and Donald sat at the breakfast table on November 19, 1978, in a stunned silence. Finally Donald said, "Are you thinking what I'm thinking? Isn't that the outfit that Clay was so enthusiastic about in his letter?" Emily replied, "Yes, I wonder if he was there."

Donald mused, "It seemed like he was planning to follow this Wonder Man of God. Where are the Pinkertons when we need them? They would be able to find out if he was or not."

Chapter 43

EPILOGUE

By 1960 the women in the family could see the futility of continuing with the tradition of Thanksgiving at the big farmhouse. There were in-laws to consider by then who also wanted to spend the holidays with their families. And taking turns every other year didn't cut the mustard, either. There was always somebody who couldn't come. There was no problem with Molly and Frank, as Frank didn't have any relatives. Ethel Grace's husband, Rob, had family in Little Rock, Arkansas. Vern's wife, Joyce, had family at Chattanooga, so they had to divide time on holidays with both families. Ruthie and Gunter weren't much of a problem, because Gunter's family lived in Perryville. So, Emily decreed that every family was on it's own for Thanksgiving, but they were going to start a Family Reunion on the first Sunday in August every year to be hosted by whoever wanted it. She knew that she and Donald would never be alone on Thanksgiving. Claudia was delighted. She was already trying to juggle her family and Evan's family, so it made it easier for her.

In 1982, Donald was 81. He was a little stooped and his white hair was very thin on top, he wore glasses and had a serious hearing problem but the eternal smile was always ready to break out when something amused him. The slight nod of his head still marked his approval of most any situation. And he still looked at Emily like she had just hung the moon. Emily was 80 and her hair was completely white. She used a cane most of the time due to her old bugaboo, arthritis. There was no pantsuit for her. She dressed in a neat dress, as ladies of her vintage should. Both she and Donald had their own teeth yet so there was no slipping of the teeth to distract when she was telling her story.

There would be 34 people attending, unless Agnes' two great-granddaughters and their families came down from Ohio like they did one year. Then there would be 4 more people-unless they brought some of their children.

Vern and Joyce were holding it this year at the big farmhouse. The kids would probably have a water fight and maybe the big kids would even get in on it. The swing was still on the oak tree across the drive and Vern had checked it all out to make sure it was safe. One thing had changed. When Ruthie moved into the house on Oakland Street in town, the fancy swing board that Donald had made her for Christmas that first year had gone with her. It now graced the swing in their oak tree in the front yard. A couple of years ago, Vern had done a makeover on the kitchen for Joyce and there was now an island and the hand-made table and chairs had been replaced by a booth, large enough for their family. There were knotty pine cupboards and a new dishwasher. The whole plumbing system had been redone and the pantry was no longer the only bathroom. In fact, there were 2 and one half bathrooms, one of them upstairs. The old root cellar and springhouse was full of cobwebs now because there was a new refrigerator and freezer system in the house. The windmill still pumped water for the stock, but the old tank was gone from the attic. Emily thought it was all pretty grand, but she couldn't recall a single instance when she didn't like the old house.

Everybody brought a dish to pass just like they always had, and the food was excellent, just like it always was. As the dessert course came around, the younger kids began to whisper and argue among themselves. The subject of the arguments was Emily herself. As was the custom, after dinner Granny would start telling stories. Each child had a favorite story and each wanted to hear their own again.

"Tell us about the time Great-Grandpa Dag and his family were going to the Strand Theater."

"No, tell us about Grandpa Dag bringing you the organ in the wagon."

"Tell us about Pops getting his hand shot off."

"I want to hear about your Mama running away with you and giving you to somebody else."

"Tell us about the Pinkertons."

"No, tell us about Uncle Joey and Uncle Frank going to the war."

"I want to hear about how Aunt Molly and Aunt Ethel Grace's dad robbed a bank and then left them with you and Granddad while he ran away from the FBI." This last didn't seem to faze the women in question in the least. It was merely family history.

Finally Emily held up her hand for silence. "I'm going to tell you today about how Granddad and I met and fell in love." She took a drink of water, cleared her throat and started out: "The year was 1931. The place could have been Anywhere USA, but in reality it was Perryville, Kentucky. We were well in to the Great Depression, although, at that time, we just called it 'hard times'. I was on my way with Joey and Ruthie to live with my sister in Redhouse, Virginia..............................."